real
CIDERMAKING
ON A SMALL SCALE

D1550679

real CIDERMAKING
ON A SMALL SCALE

An Introduction to Producing Cider at Home

By Michael Pooley & John Lomax

FOX CHAPEL
PUBLISHING

Copyright © Michael Pooley and John Lomax, 1999, 2011.

First published in the United Kingdom by Nexus Special Interest Ltd., 1999.

First published in North America in 2011, updated and revised, by Fox Chapel Publishing, 1970 Broad Street, East Petersburg, PA 17520.

ISBN 978-1-56523-604-2

The photos featured on pages 10, 19, 25, 33, 64, 66, and 105 are courtesy of Barbara Henry.

Library of Congress Cataloging-in-Publication Data

Pooley, Michael, 1947-

 Real cidermaking on a small scale : an introduction to producing cider at home / Michael Pooley and John Lomax. -- Updated and rev.

   p. cm.

Includes index.

ISBN 978-1-56523-604-2 (pbk.)

1. Cider. I. Lomax, John, 1950- II. Title.

TP563.P66 2011

663'.63--dc23

2011013267

To learn more about the other great books from Fox Chapel Publishing, or to find a retailer near you, call toll-free 800-457-9112 or visit us at *www.FoxChapelPublishing.com*.

Note to Authors: We are always looking for talented authors to write new books. Please send a brief letter describing your idea to Acquisition Editor, 1970 Broad Street, East Petersburg, PA 17520.

Printed in China
First printing: November 2011

CONTENTS

1

INTRODUCTION

"Oh, not cidermaking again already?" we protest. "All that cutting up and pounding of apples! We've still got the bruises on our hands from last year!"

(But secretly we like it!)

A number of things inspired this practical guide to small-scale cidermaking. The hope is this guide will provide anyone who is at least faintly interested in the craft with the skills and incentive to turn apples—especially those that might otherwise go to waste—into a delicious drink, while at the same time helping to stimulate the further cultivation and use of the fruit.

One thing leads to another. As more and more people begin to make cider, so thoughts of shaping the idea into a wider community enterprise with small community orchards and perhaps even a community press will grow. The apple is at home in any temperate climate, but compared to thirty or forty years ago, many varieties having become exhausted or eliminated through wholesale loss of orchards, resulting in the need to promote apple culture. The organization Common Ground has probably done the most in recent years to remind people of the enormous richness of their apple cultures and the threats posed by large-scale agriculture and modern retailing patterns, creating a resurgence of interest in the fruit. "Apple Day" in Britain (October 21) was started by Common Ground and has now entered the calendar as a fixed date in celebration of this culture. It is hugely popular, so much so that the idea is already being adopted in many other countries around the world. In the United States, there are apple festivals held locally in communities throughout the country, and October is dedicated as National Apple Month to support the health benefits of apples and apple products.

Such trends testify to the apple's importance, of which cider is just one vital strand. Until recently, however, the process of real cidermaking has been neglected, leading to a poor commercial product. Now there is a revival in the real product, and the hope is this book can make its contribution to the process.

On the following pages, you will find plans and information needed to build a sturdy press, the skills and confidence to make real cider, and a sustaining idea that to do so at this level is to continue an ancient rural craft. And you will have fun doing it! Small-scale cidermaking can be a wonderful communal activity—low-tech and in need of people. We should celebrate the fact that it is labor intensive. The physical labor in cidermaking itself is satisfying, because it is earthy, shared, varied, and directed to some splendid product, while the occasion—whether you live in an urban or rural environment—is full of rich social and recreational possibilities for adults and children alike engaged upon a common enterprise.

Whether you have fruit from just one or two trees in the garden, or a large harvest of apples each fall from a small orchard, or even access to much larger supplies, the hope is that this book will inspire you to make cider. Good cidermaking!

2

A WORD ON APPLES

*The wild crab is solitary, found in woods or roadside hedges.
Its blossom is lovely as any, but the smell of its fallen fruit on
a winter's day walk, when thoughts of apples have long been
left behind, is so delicious it might tempt you, as legend has
it. Would you bite into a crab apple? It would bite you back
with interest!*

The apple is an astonishing creation. Sow a small seed and each time it would
grow to bear a different variety. The ancestry of the cultivated fruit we know
today as *Malus pumila domestica*, leads back through the ages to the wild
crab from the Caucasus region of modern Georgia. Thousands of years of
hybridization and grafting experiments by human beings, along with processes
of natural selection, have resulted in a fruit of such rich genetic makeup that the
number of possible varieties is quite staggering.

Everything flows from this complex history. The apple is quite exceptional
among fruits in having such diversity of shape, color, texture, flavor, and
cropping season, considering all of the varieties involved. There are more
cultivars of the apple than any other fruit of similar importance, and although
most are at home in a cool temperate climate, few places in the world—barring
the tropics themselves—are unwelcoming of at least one variety or another.

In Britain today, hundreds of different examples still thrive, and over
the centuries as many as 6,000 or more have been bred or discovered. The
likelihood, however, of our sown pip ever yielding a variety of any worth is
extremely small, for those that we have come to value for this reason or that,
adapted to this locality or that, have been arrived at by the amateur grower's or
the professional plant breeder's art of ruthless selection and rejection. Those
we do value are sweet to eat, cook well, make excellent cider, resist disease
and frosts, crop heavily, are aesthetic of shape and color, and so on. The vast
majority of the many varieties still to be found in Britain are local in the sense
of being distinctive to an area, or even unique to a parish or neighborhood
according to the nature of the soil, climate, and the circumstances that brought
them into being at all.

A collection of apples ready for washing prior to cutting up, milling, and pressing

The long tradition of selecting for new qualities in the apple continues today. There are many examples of successful modern cultivars, but the truth is the best varieties are the old ones. And behind each one, perhaps intimated in the name, lies the story: the chance discovery, the painstaking work, the labor of love. It is due to this work and dedication that we have such varieties as Ashmead's Kernel, Cox's Orange Pippin, or that most famous of culinary apples, the Bramley's Seedling, raised in a Nottinghamshire cottage garden by Betsy Brailsford sometime between 1809 and 1813. Where the seed came from isn't known, but the original tree is still there, thriving.

Just as rich as the apple itself is the body of literature, music, art, folk stories, recipes, sayings, and myths that have come to surround the fruit. Its very ordinariness is its richness, the fact that it is such a commonplace thing the reason why it touches people, enters so extensively into the language and culture, and has come to be used to symbolize so many different aspects of our lives.

The apple often embodies a kind of homeliness *as a Kerry Pippin to crack and crunch*, a comeliness as the tree that *leans down low at Linden Lee*, or a panacea of good health (at least in keeping the doctor away). It has entered into the language, resulting in phrases like: wrinkle with age as an *apple-john*, they are *crabbed* of personality, or I enjoy a way life that is often *sweet on one side, bitter on the other*. There

are also those cherished as the Psalmist's *apple of an eye*. Some things are just in *apple-pie order*, and some offers are as tempting (and perhaps as dire if taken up) as Eve's. Some insights are as ordinary and profound as Newton's supposed route to gravity, and some historical figures as memorable as William Tell. The symbols and stories are seemingly endless.

Apple blossom on a large Bramley's Seedling tree

The etymology of the word apple is as fascinating as it is unresolved. The major European languages, apart from the Romance languages, have words for the fruit that are prefixed with ap-, ab-, or similar alternatives, but all curiously seem to predate or find no origin in any Indo-European root. (The Arabic al- seems suggestive, but it is difficult to establish any credible route.) That other Indo-European-rooted language, Latin, has an alternative etymology, giving us *malus*, derived from the Greek *mailon*. Just as the word cider itself formerly denoted fermented drinks from a whole range of fruits, or even Eve's offer from the garden of a fruit rather than an apple, so *mailon* appears not so much a cognate in Greek of apple as the generic for fruit, though the word is still retained in English, specifically in melon.

3
CIDERMAKING HISTORY

Little wonder there are so many alcoholic drinks. Sugars and starches in fruits and cereals are disposed to ferment naturally and the formation of cider is no exception. It is possible that cider has existed in some form for almost as long as there have been apples—say, a few thousand years.

Seventeenth-century milling machine

Perhaps something of the real antiquity of cider is held in the widespread tradition of its communal drinking. Nineteenth-century photographs and other archival material show that at harvest or haymaking—the two most important times in the farm calendar— laborers would regularly quench their thirst with their part-wage payment of cider. The custom was that the cider was poured into a common drinking cup and handed to each man in turn, going round in a circle, clockwise. This manner of sharing out the drink in turn using the same vessel seems an age-old custom or rite. It is still found in some traditional cider-producing countries, such as Asturias (in northern Spain) and Normandy. There, the cider is shared at the table during mealtime. Indeed, in Asturias, the meal itself cannot be commenced until each member has first finished his small glass of cider, always to be drunk down in one go, as a symbol of sharing and kind of blessing of labor and the harvest. Perhaps there are resonances here of something very old. Certainly, for a long time, the apple tree itself was regarded as sacred.

There can be no doubt that cidermaking really grew up in those cooler northwest regions of Europe, where the vine finally gives way to the apple: northern Spain, Wiesbaden in Germany, Normandy and Brittany in France, and particularly the southern and western counties of England. In time, through emigration, the skills were exported to all those other temperate regions of the world in the northern and southern hemispheres where cider came to be made and is still appreciated today.

Although the first official references in England to cider come from royal accounts in the thirteenth century, cider has certainly been with us for a lot longer than that, predating the Romans, and also likely predating the making of ale from barley and certainly beer.

While the fortunes of the drink seem to have waxed and waned at the aristocrat's table, the tradition of making and drinking cider elsewhere in England and Wales where the apple thrived remained strong throughout the centuries. It appears to have reached its greatest popularity in the seventeenth and eighteenth centuries, when it supplanted ale as the preferred drink. Among the upper classes, some of the best keeved (fermented) ciders were compared to the finest French wines. John Evelyn published his great treatise, *Pomona*, on the subject of cider and all related subjects in 1670, and during the following centuries, the publications on orcharding and cidermaking techniques continued to flow, indicating just how important the drink had become. In fact, the popularity of the drink remained strong, even through difficult times in the nineteenth century, and has only declined substantially in the last several decades. Each of the farms and those country estates with their own home farm and orchards would have had their cider mill and press, sometimes in their own building (the mill house), and the volumes of cider produced each year meant they were usually more than self-sufficient in the drink.

Chronicling the rich traditions surrounding every aspect of cider in Britain didn't really begin until the twentieth century, and even then, most has been accomplished since the Second World War. It draws upon a rich seam of archival material, mostly from the nineteenth century, corresponding to a time when the society slowly became more literate, increasingly industrialized (bringing profound changes to people's lives and customs), and saw the advent of such inventions as photography. In that century, and even up to the First World War and beyond, we discover the importance of cider to a rural agricultural society, where it was made largely for consumption by the farm household

A small cider press is perfect for producing a few gallons of delicious cider.

and farm workers. At that time, cidermaking was so basic and unobtrusive a practice, it rarely even entered the farm accounts.

Technical changes, particularly the replacement of the wooden screw in the cider press with the first cast iron screws in the late-eighteenth century, and the development of the much smaller scratter mill for the old horse-drawn mechanical means of crushing apples, produced another interesting scion of the tradition: the travelling cidermaker of the nineteenth century. He would travel about between farms that lay on the margins of the main apple-growing areas that didn't have the means to support the necessary equipment, and also from inn to inn. In the short cidermaking season, he would extract juice that the farmer and innkeeper would then ferment for the needs of workers or customers.

The latest chapter in the story of cider really belongs to the growth of a few large manufacturers of cider. Toward the end of the nineteenth century, in response to the massive urbanization occurring and a commensurate decrease in the numbers of agricultural laborers due to the scale of mechanization, the needs and purposes behind the old farm-based tradition of making cider steadily began to die. The process continued well into the twentieth century, and saw perhaps another dramatic stage of decline with that great turning point in British society, World War I. After that, while the tradition lingered on here and there and even survived in isolated spots beyond World War II, to all intents and purposes, the tradition was dead. And yet, perhaps we are already witnessing something of the proverbial phoenix. While it is certainly the factory-produced cider that dominates the market today, perhaps the renaissance of interest in real cider that has arisen in the last few years will, in the forms of the small-scale producer and the domestic and community production of cider, come to represent the vigor of a new variety grafted onto the old stock.

4

BUILDING THE PRESS

It is said that after World War I, much of the farm cidermaking equipment in Britain was systematically bought up by a number of the growing commercial concerns. The farmers were only too pleased to accept a little much-needed cash to get rid of equipment that was simply rusting and rotting way. Once purchased, the milling machines and presses were smashed up and burned, so they could never be used again.

First comes the cider press. As George Borrow remarked, "The effort in learning a foreign language is as nothing compared to the pleasure that follows from using it." So it is with cider presses. Making the press—a simple and inexpensive matter—should be thought of as acquiring a piece of equipment as indispensable to the household or community in its way as, say, an oven, television, or car. The design of the press shown at the end of the chapter is extremely sturdy, and is based upon one type of traditional farm press. Once made, it will last a lifetime and beyond. It may even turn out to be a family heirloom. The press is a scaled-down version of a simple single-screw press, comprising three main components:

- A heavy steel screw plunger mechanism obtained by mail order from a woodworking machinery supplier that might require some simple modification by any local metalworking shop
- A bolted timber frame and base
- A slatted box of approximately 10.5 quarts (10 liters) capacity to contain the apple pulp and tray

The finished press measures some 30 in. (762 mm.) high by 24 in. (610 mm.) wide and should give up to a third or half a gallon (about 2 liters) of juice to each pressing, depending on how well the apples are pulped.

Full instructions for building your own press can be found at the end of this chapter on four illustrated sheets. For a consideration of other designs of presses suitable for producing much larger volumes of juice, see Chapter 9.

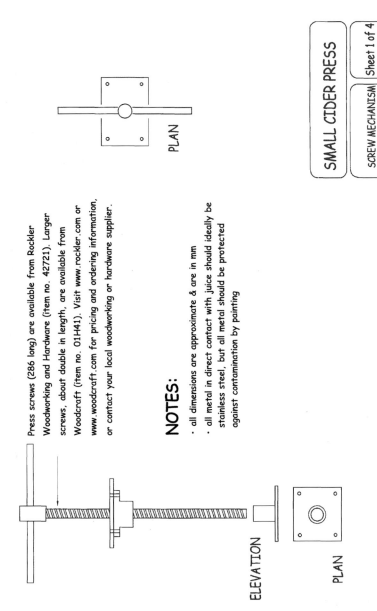

NOTES:

Press screws (286 long) are available from Rockler Woodworking and Hardware (item no. 42721). Larger screws, about double in length, are available from Woodcraft (item no. 01H41). Visit www.rockler.com or www.woodcraft.com for pricing and ordering information, or contact your local woodworking or hardware supplier.

· all dimensions are approximate & are in mm
· all metal in direct contact with juice should ideally be stainless steel, but all metal should be protected against contamination by painting

PLAN

ELEVATION

PLAN

SMALL CIDER PRESS

SCREW MECHANISM   Sheet 1 of 4

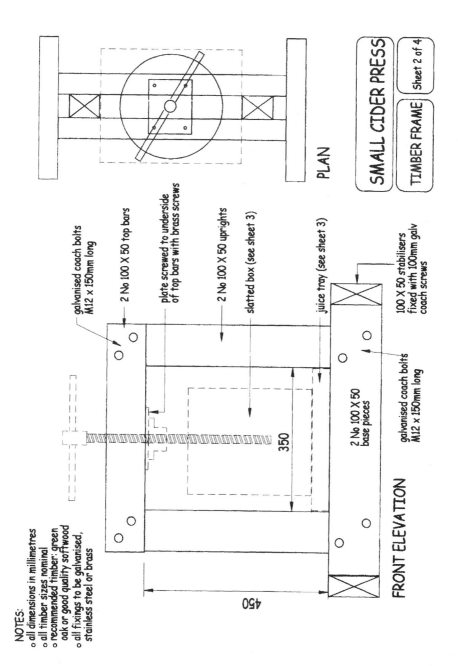

PLAN

SMALL CIDER PRESS   Sheet 2 of 4

TIMBER FRAME

galvanised coach bolts M12 x 150mm long

2 No 100 X 50 top bars

plate screwed to underside of top bars with brass screws

2 No 100 X 50 uprights

slatted box (see sheet 3)

juice tray (see sheet 3)

100 X 50 stabilisers fixed with 100mm galv coach screws

2 No 100 X 50 base pieces

galvanised coach bolts M12 x 150mm long

350

450

FRONT ELEVATION

NOTES:
o all dimensions in millimetres
o all timber sizes nominal
o recommended timber: green oak or good quality softwood
o all fixings to be galvanised, stainless steel or brass

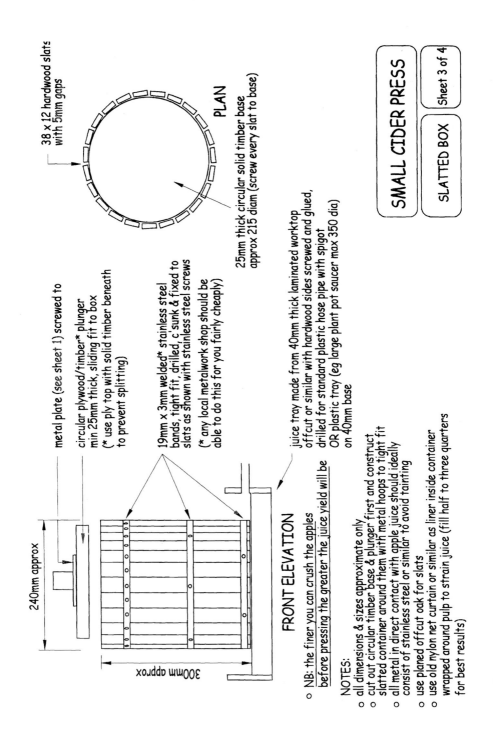

38 x 12 hardwood slats with 5mm gaps

PLAN

25mm thick circular solid timber base approx 215 diam (screw every slat to base)

metal plate (see sheet 1) screwed to

circular plywood/timber* plunger min 25mm thick, sliding fit to box (* use ply top with solid timber beneath to prevent splitting)

19mm x 3mm welded* stainless steel bands, tight fit, drilled, c'sunk & fixed to slats as shown with stainless steel screws

(* any local metalwork shop should be able to do this for you fairly cheaply)

juice tray made from 40mm thick laminated worktop offcut or similar with hardwood sides screwed and glued, drilled for standard plastic hose pipe with spigot OR plastic tray (eg large plant pot saucer max 350 dia) on 40mm base

240mm approx

300mm approx

FRONT ELEVATION

o NB: the finer you can crush the apples before pressing the greater the juice yield will be

NOTES:
o all dimensions & sizes approximate only
o cut out circular timber base & plunger first and construct slatted container around them with metal hoops to tight fit
o all metal in direct contact with apple juice should ideally consist of stainless steel or similar to avoid tainting
o use planed offcut oak for slats
o use old nylon net curtain or similar as liner inside container wrapped around pulp to strain juice (fill half to three quarters for best results)

SMALL CIDER PRESS

SLATTED BOX   Sheet 3 of 4

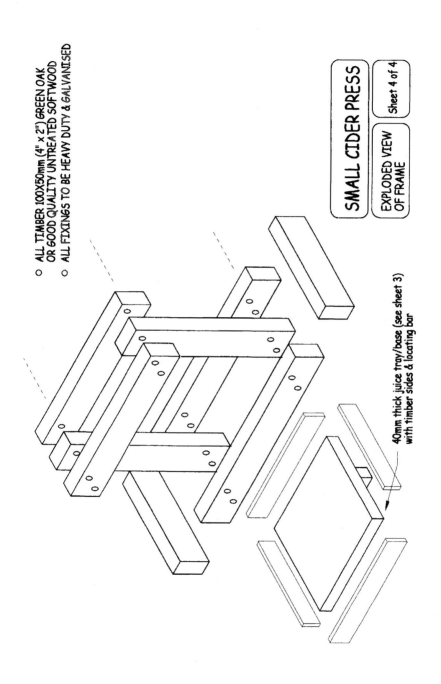

o ALL TIMBER 100X50mm (4" x 2") GREEN OAK
  OR GOOD QUALITY UNTREATED SOFTWOOD
o ALL FIXINGS TO BE HEAVY DUTY & GALVANISED

SMALL CIDER PRESS

EXPLODED VIEW OF FRAME

Sheet 4 of 4

40mm thick juice tray/base (see sheet 3)
with timber sides & locating bar

5

AN AUTUMN DAY'S CIDERMAKING

It's Pick & Mix

Wash & Chop

Crush & Press

Ferment…Store…Serve

Small-scale might mean producing anything from 1 to 2 gallons of cider up to a few hundred. Here, the term is used to suggest a scale of cidermaking that employs only the most basic low-tech equipment, including the press.

Exactly how much juice is extracted in, say, a day of cidermaking will of course depend on the effort, but using such equipment, roughly 20 lb. (9 kg.) of apples convert to 5 quarts (4.5 liters) of juice. In our experience, 100 to 150 quarts (95-142 liters) of juice in a day would be considered very fair.

Those who would like to generate much larger quantities than this (perhaps thinking of retailing it) will necessarily have to secure a sufficient supply of apples, be prepared to set aside a number of days extracting the juice,

Crushing the apples before pressing

and/or invest in larger more sophisticated equipment (as discussed in Chapter 9). For some people, the pleasure of a day or a season of making cider is a domestic or even individual affair, but cidermaking at this level, unlike beer and winemaking at home, is ideally a craft shared out among a group of people. Anywhere between half a dozen and a dozen people (with children, all the better) makes an ideal number, each bringing a contribution to the pile of apples, and at the end of the day, taking away a share of the juice to be fermented at home. Clearly, if two or more presses are available, then larger numbers could work, as part of a small community day activity, for example, but if the event is being hosted by an individual or a family, they will need to be aware of keeping numbers manageable.

The most important aspect to the philosophy behind small-scale cidermaking is the celebration of the fact it is low-tech and labor intensive. Therein lies its secret. The product is ultimately delicious and wholesome, because at every stage, it is completely touched by the human hand, unlike many modern commercial concoctions that try to avoid, if at all possible, going anywhere near a human being.

The pleasures and the satisfactions in making cider at this level lie as much in the diversity of the stages involved in getting the juice as the fermentation process to the final product. There is the gathering, mixing, washing, preparing, and quartering of the apples with much banter across the table and intense discussions as to how the processes might be sped up with better technology. There is a good deal of enjoyment to be had, not least by children, in the pounding of the quartered apples to crush them, using a simple pole as a pestle (more sophisticated alternatives are available if preferred). Finally, there is the satisfaction of the actual pressing, watching the apple juice come pouring out into its receptacle.

Tasting the juice is an experience in its own right, and to observe the reaction of the most ardent skeptic, who, after much urging from others, finally agrees to sample the thick muddy liquid, is as amusing as it is invariable. The face becomes suffused with astonishment and undisguised pleasure as to how delicious it is.

The whole process is, of course, extremely inefficient, at least, that is, if judged by the mean calculus of how much juice is extracted from how much time and energy is put in. But it is wonderfully efficient in terms of how much sharing takes place, how much fun is to be had, and in the exercise, wit, humor, and gossip generated. It's as "refreshing of the spirit" as the drinking of the cider will be in its own way in due course.

Choose one of those lovely crisp sunny days in October, or even November, for your cidermaking day. A certain amount of planning will be necessary beforehand, but you will be blessed with fine weather anyway, because cidermaking is a virtuous thing. If you are doing it communally, make sure everyone has had plenty of notice and is well prepared. Food will be required (we normally arrange for the family hosting the event to supply lunch): extracting apple juice all day can build up a furious hunger. Drink, too, is completely indispensable, because what you are embarking upon is effectively a daylong party—a working party, and thirsty work at that. Copious quantities of wine, beer, or even some of last year's cider (if you have any left) will help ensure the wit, repartee, and gossip begin to flow in line with the juice. Any questions of Puritan guilt about enjoying yourself too much may be safely discounted, because you will be earning the enjoyment at a fair old rate of demijohns and 5-gallon drums of pressed apple juice.

The equipment needed for small-scale cidermaking is simple:

- The basket press with nylon sieve or square of net curtain or the volume press with cloths and wooden racks for cheese (see Chapter 9)

- Tub (e.g., plastic trashcan; avoid metal containers, except stainless steel) filled with water into which apples are poured and washed

- Table upon which to cut out rot and quarter the apples

- A couple of old 15-20 quart (13.5-18 liter) plastic buckets for carrying apples to the table and for disposal of discarded apples

* White food-grade 20-25 quart (18-22.5 liter) plastic bucket/bin in which the quartered apples are crushed (see Chapter 8)

* A couple of pestle poles (see Chapter 8)

* Simple scratting mill (optional: see Chapter 8).

* Fermentation vessels: glass demijohns, large white food-grade fermentation bins, or anything else suitable

* Sundries: cotton wool, cloths, fermentation locks, sodium metabisulfite, etc.

* Large plastic trashcan or plastic trashcan liners into which the spent apple pulp (pomace) is put before composting, etc.

* Access to an outside tap and, if possible, pressure hose for filling tubs and cleaning equipment at end of day

6

THE RIGHT MIX OF APPLES

First catch your apple.

Then another…

Many potentially good ciders, and certainly a great deal of effort, are spoiled for want of having spent a bit of time at the outset in getting a balanced mix of apples. So often the would-be cidermaker simply gathers up what apples are there and gets straight into pounding and pressing. This chapter, however, makes a simple plea to spend a little time in securing, if possible, a good mix of apples. The juice and the final product will reward handsomely the investment of the time.

There are many varieties of genuine cider apples, some of long pedigree, such as that most famous all-rounder, Kingston Black, along with the likes of Tom Putt, Foxwhelp, and Brown Snout. And what of "Slack Ma Girdle" for a name—an old sweet Devon variety perhaps alluding to cider's reputation for keeping you slim. The variety is still available. Modern cultivars continue the tradition of both flavor and lovely names, such as Yarlington Mill, Dabinett, and Chisel Jersey. Discussing the tradition of cider apples and the naming of apples could happily occupy another book in its own right.

Cider Fruit

Cider fruit needs to be considered, however, to discover what makes a really good cider. Traditionally, such apples might very well have been eaten or used for cooking, but were often especially valued for making cider. They are most closely related to the wild crab apple, often appearing unattractively blotched and scabby, but having the characteristics in their juice that make them excellent for cider. The juice has a sweetness and acidity and a high level of tannin that imparts a bitterness and dryness in the mouth, referred to as astringency. It is these three ingredients found in real cider apples that confer a range and complexity of flavors to the cider and are at the heart of a really good cider.

Depending on the balance of tannin to sweetness or acidity, cider apples are generally divided into two categories: bittersweets and bittersharps. These days, bittersweets are the preferred type of cider apples used most often commercially in Britain. Sweets and sharps are two further low-tannin categories used in describing cider fruit. All other apples that are not typified as cider varieties—but can still be used to make cider—are referred to as dessert apples (eaters), culinary apples (cookers), and those that are dual-purpose. The following table gives the compositions of some typical apple juices along with a target or ideal juice composition for the making of excellent ciders.

Consideration of these values leads us to a further interesting characteristic of some cider fruit that is more than noteworthy. Those cultivars that are regarded as producing the very finest ciders in terms of body and flavor are known as vintage quality. The term is difficult to define precisely in biochemical terms, but just as with varieties of grapes, hops, or barley, there are some apple cultivars that possess superior attributes of sugar, acid, tannin, and a host of other subtle qualities that affect the rate and nature of the fermentation, and therefore the quality of the resultant cider. Compared to the great number of (still available) cider apple varieties, the number of vintage examples is relatively few, but in cider-making circles, there appears to be a consensus as to those cultivars that have vintage quality. Some of the more important examples with their characteristics are listed on the following chart.

THE COMPOSITION OF SOME APPLE JUICES. APPROXIMATE % VALUES EXPRESSED AS MASS (G.)/100 ML. OF JUICE.

Property	Typical pure sweet	Typical pure sharp	Typical bittersweet	Juice target for excellent ciders
Sugar	13	11	15	15
Malic acid	0.2	1	0.2	0.4
Tannin	0.15	0.15	0.3	0.2

VINTAGE CIDER CULTIVARS

Cultivar	Category	Cider characteristics
Browns Apple	Pure sharp	Light, sharp, and fruity cider
Fair Maid of Devon	Pure sharp	Excellent juice volume, sharp and fruity cider
Kingston Black	Medium bittersweet	Full-bodied, spicy, regarded as the finest vintage variety
Stoke Red	Medium bittersweet	Full-bodied, fruity, excellent single-variety cider
Broxwood Foxwhelp	Medium bittersweet	Full-bodied, very distinctive aroma and flavor
Ashton Brown Jersey	Full bittersweet	Good quality, astringent cider
Sercombes Natural	Mild bittersweet	Soft tannin cider
Somerset Redstreak	Mild bittersweet	Good body, soft tannin cider, useful blender
Dabinett	Full bittersweet	Full-bodied, soft tannin, indispensable for blending
Yarlington Mill	Mild bittersweet	Good body, fruity, soft tannin, superior cider
Major	Full bittersweet	Fruity, average quality, useful for blending
Harry Masters Jersey	Medium bittersweet	Soft astringent tannin, very good single-varietal cider
Medaille D'Or	Full bittersweet	High levels of soft tannin, good quality cider
Sweet Coppin	Pure sweet	Very useful vintage cider
Sweet Alford	Pure sweet	One of the most valuable all-round vintage ciders

At a small-scale or domestic level, most people will, of course, simply use whatever apples are to hand, and that is as it should be. Any apples will do: early or late windfalls, apples shaken down, handpicked, begged, or borrowed. However, the best apples to use are the ripest ones, because they will have the highest sugar content and produce the richest and most alcoholic ciders.

Apples will begin to fall in September and are best piled up, say, on a plastic sheet, or better still, sacking, on the ground, grass, or orchard floor until you choose the opportune day to commence cidermaking. Cover the top of the pile with old carpet or sacking to protect it from the worst of the weather. In the pile, the apples will continue to ripen, soften, and begin to smell very sweet. Add to it from whatever source. If the main bulk of the apples are from late-maturing sources, then you will obviously be choosing a day in November to make cider, but everything else being equal, October is really the month for it. It has a further advantage, alluded to more than once in this book, that, if fermented a little faster, then bottled or otherwise stored, the cider will be ready by Christmas, and a glass of chilled cider in a house sometimes singing with the warmth of Christmas preparations, or an offering of mulled cider when coming in from a frosted evening of carols, is a pleasure indeed.

If your pile, or tump, of apples is likely to be left for some time, it is advisable at periodic intervals to turn it over, removing those apples that are brown and rotten due to the *botrytis* fungus. The rate of infection of sound apples can be very rapid (see Appendix 6).

We can aspire to as rich and balanced a juice as possible by considering for a moment what is involved. Learn to recognize the culinary type, such as the Bramley, or other green cookers, which are rich in acid, and the dessert apple or eaters, which will be relatively sweet.

You may also have access to apples that, upon tasting, demonstrate a fair degree of astringency. If this appears to be lacking from all of your apples, add a small ration of crab apples to the mix to supply the tannin. Try to aim for a mix of these types and spend a few minutes physically mixing them up  before cleaning and chopping and preparing the apple pulp prior to pressing. If you are uncertain at the apple mixing-up stage whether you have got the right balance, then wait until you've pressed out some juice and taste it. It will always be delicious, but if it is demonstrably sweet, while lacking distinctive acidity on the palate, then you will need to add more cookers to the mix as you go along. You can adjust an overly acidic juice by piling in more of the dessert apples with the next press. Try to avoid a preponderance of cooking apples in the mix. This is because once the apple sugars have been fermented to alcohol, the acidity will be a very dominant feature of the resulting cider, and this may even experience more difficulty in clearing.

Blending Juices

An alternative to blending the fruit prior to pressing is for the cidermaker to press individual cultivars, assess the nature of the resultant juice from each, and then blend to arrive at the desired balanced juice before fermentation (there may or may not be a need to make further adjustments to the juice as discussed in Chapter 9). Many cidermakers operate this way, arguing they have greater control over the blending process in consequence. If you intend following this procedure, clearly you will need to keep your fruit in separate piles. One of the great advantages of this approach is you will get to know the characteristics of your individual cider cultivars and their juices.

Blending Ciders

It is even the case that a great many cidermakers (especially those retailing cider) do not even bother to blend either fruit or juice at this stage. Instead, they press and ferment single varietal ciders and leave any necessary blending to the final cider stage. Once again, this is an excellent opportunity to relate the individual cultivar to its cider characteristics and you may wish to adopt this approach. However, in general, if you are a relative beginner to the craft, it is probably advisable to blend at the fruit or juice stage and leave cider blending itself until you have gained more experience. Blending ciders is considered much more fully in Chapter 11.

Conclusion

The following example will illustrate the main thrust of this chapter. Recently, we tasted a dry still cider made, as it turned out, from twenty-one different varieties of cidermaking apples—many of them venerable indeed, and all with the most delicious of names printed on a splendid label. The product, alas, was bland and hugely disappointing. Why? Almost certainly because of a basic failure to establish a sound blend and a balance between the contrasting types of apple that make a good cider. In the same way, although the products are much vaunted, many people find the fashion for single-variety ciders disappointing. Apart from notable exceptions, such as the Kingston Black or other bittersweet vintage cider apples, many single varieties will tend to produce a cider with none of the heady aroma, full flavor, and all those other subtleties and nuances that should be the feature of a traditional cider. As with people, so with apples for cider—the more contrasting types you have together, the richer the event.

Cutting out rot and quartering apples prior to milling or crushing them

7

WASHING AND PREPARING THE APPLES

When you have chosen a cidermaking day (or days) and are ready to press the fruit, gather it to the site, discard all fruit that is in any way moldy or excessively bruised (see Appendix 6), then, if you haven't done it already, try to establish a good blend of the different apples you have according to the principles set out in the previous chapter. (Alternatively, you may wish to treat the preparation and subsequent pressing of the apples on a single-variety basis.)

Pour the apples in batches into a large bucket or tub of cold water and give them a thorough wash around, removing soil, bloom, surface sliminess, and any rotten apples (these will usually sink). It is important to wash the apples thoroughly at this stage to remove any enteric bacteria, such as those originating, say, from animal-grazed orchards, and also to minimize those wild yeasts on the skin, which may contribute to cider taint such as mousiness (see Chapter 12).

Change the water at periodic intervals or use a hose to fill up with fresh water. Transfer the clean apples to a table, where they should be quartered. Cut out the worst of any rot and bruising, but do not be over fastidious or attempt to remove cores and pips as some beginning the craft believe is necessary. As any child knows who has ever bitten on a pip and explored it, there is a range of delicious flavors to be experienced. It was this that the old cidermakers, using a mechanical means of crushing and pulverizing the apple prior to pressing, regarded as adding another distinctive dimension to the flavor of the final cider, and which they asserted was much reduced with the development of the scratting mill.

Apart from these obvious preliminaries, you can use the apples as they come, and this stage should be done relatively quickly and without in any way being onerous.

8

MILLING AND CRUSHING THE APPLES

The pressure required to extract even a fraction of the juice from a whole apple is remarkable. For this reason it is necessary to mill and/or crush the apples beforehand. The more completely this is done, the more juice will be extracted when pressing. Be aware that in a particularly dry year, when the apples may have far less juice in them than normal, they will need to soften more than usual in the stacked pile prior to pressing and the quartered apples will need to be crushed a bit more thoroughly to extract as much juice as possible.

Mincers, known as scratters or scratting mills, are available commercially and can be operated by hand or by electricity. If you find cidermaking to your taste in a big way, you may wish to invest in a small domestic model. Some people make good use of garden shredders for the purpose of milling apples, however, for most people the easiest—and by far the cheapest— approach to arriving at the apple pulp is to physically crush the quartered apples using a 2-yard (about 2 meter) length of timber, approximately 4-5 in. (10-12 cm.) square, or if you have access to woodland, a pole

A typical scratting mill

of any timber of similar diameter. If you want to make this even more efficient, drill laterally through the pole 2-3 in. (6-8 cm.) from the top, and insert a short length of 1-in. (25 mm.) dowel to provide a handle on either side. Insert another handle(s) lower down if you want to be thoroughly child-friendly.

Now place about an 8-in. (20 cm.) deep pile of quartered apples in a food-grade plastic bucket (white or clear is best, avoid highly colored) or a wooden pail, and pulverize them with the pole. Make sure you place the plastic bucket on a flat level piece of ground, free of protruding stones, to avoid splitting the base of the bucket as you work. Stainless steel vessels can also be used, but otherwise avoid any metal container, since apple juice is an acidic liquid that both attacks and is tainted by metal.

It is best if two people work together to crush the apples, using a method called double-splodge or double-bash. This builds up to a rhythmic pounding similar to the work of pounding maize and other cereals. Indeed, in the best sense of the word, there is something primitive and peculiarly satisfying, especially for the child in us, in operating one of these poles. Comparisons have also shown that although extremely low-tech, at this level, the pole is as efficient at getting the apple into the requisite state for pressing as the small scratting mill (although even if using this, the milled apple should be pounded somewhat afterwards anyway). The apple pulp should be nice and sloppy. It will also benefit in flavor from the fact that many of the pips have become crushed.

On a historical and recreational note, you may, if you feel so inclined, develop songs to accompany the pounding and bashing of the apples. As in the best tradition of repetitive rhythmic physical work (sailors with their sea shanties, for example), songs aid the labor and undoubtedly extract more juice (probably in trying to remember the words, you forget what you are doing). At least it is another opportunity to sing, and then there is the sense of feeling connections, actually physically living a part of a long tradition. Almost certainly, before the horse-drawn stone mill wheel entered the scene (let alone the scratting mill), our earliest medieval forebears would have used the same sort of poles or pounding devices. To be doing precisely the same thing now as a part of the same craft of cidermaking is to be rather more than just historically in touch with those ancestors and a little part of their lives across the hundreds of intervening years.

9

PRESSING THE APPLE PULP

"I remember we didn't have a press for two or three years.
You get desperate, don't you? We used the spin cycle of the
automatic washing machine, putting the apple pulp in a
pillowcase and producing batches of 20-30 gallons of juice
without any difficulty. Mind you, we made sure the pipes
were well clear of soap beforehand!"

It is amazing the length some cidermakers will go to get their juice. If using a small basket press of the type described in Chapter 4, set it up at a convenient height so you don't have to bend much. Inside the slatted box, you will need to fit a nylon sieve bag or a large square of nylon net curtain, which is then folded over the pulp. You should avoid net curtain in which the weave is either too large or too fine, but otherwise, any will do, and, provided it is washed out and dried at the end of the cidermaking session, will give good service for years.

Load up the sieve bag or net curtain, previously placed on the inside of the basket, by scooping up apple pulp (best and stickiest by hand) between half and two-thirds full for maximum extraction of juice. Turn the thread, making sure you engage it in the press plate on top of the pulp. The juice runs out between the slats into the collection tray, and then, by means of a funnel or length of plastic hose, into a suitable container. It is most convenient to press this juice directly into the fermentation container(s), either glass demijohns or 25-30 quart (22.5-28 liter) food-grade plastic fermentation bins that can take a fermentation lock. Make certain the vessels are thoroughly clean before allowing the apple juice to run into them (see "Preparing the Fermentation Vessels" in Chapter 10).

Higher Volumes (50 gallons or more)

If you have access to large supplies of fruit—plentiful farm fruit or from your own orchard perhaps—you may be intending to produce much higher volumes of cider than are practically possible with the basket press described so far. You will need to build or purchase a press that's design and capacity reflects your ambitions. There are a number of different types available from commercial suppliers, or even from farms, where an old press might have lain abandoned for years and can be bought cheaply enough. This is particularly true in Normandy and Brittany, where there are many good presses to be had that have remained in farm outbuildings or dedicated ciderhouses for years. It is simply a question of getting to know of their existence. Sometimes it is useful to advertise online. Usually, once it is known you are looking for a press, word gets round, and someone somewhere will point you in the right direction.

One common type of large-volume press uses a central screw with a ratchet and arm mechanism. This is a relatively simple design and easy to operate. Harder work, but even sturdier in the long run, is the twinscrew press with a head block (a beam of oak usually) supported in collars that fit into special grooves in the nuts used to screw the head block down onto the pulp below. Each nut has three or four fixed wrought "wings" that are first turned by hand, each screw alternately, and when the going gets tough, by a lever arm. A third class of press can be made very simply using a hydraulic car jack, nothing more actually being needed than a fixed beam or joist above and against which the jack can push.

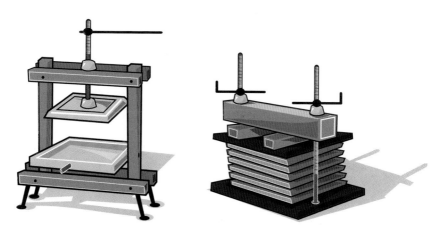

Large-volume presses like these will allow you to produce greater quantities of cider.

However, all of these types of press require that the apple pulp is piled up underneath—no mean feat given that it is far too sloppy to stay in one place. The technique is to bind up the pulp in some way. Traditionally, mixing pulp with straw to make what was called a mock did this. More commonly, the pulp was carefully folded into medium-sized mesh sacking or cloths known as hairs and built up to make a cheese. The term is still used nowadays, and in operating these larger presses, every cidermaker takes pleasure in building up the cheese or rack—an essential stage in the craft before obtaining the juice. Straw and sacking have long been replaced by terylene or other polyester cloths that are filled with a few inches of apple pulp before each cloth is carefully folded over and separated by good hardwood, semi-hardwood, or plastic racks until the cheese is built up.

The final stage requires placing a heavy board on top of the cheese to spread the weight before applying gentle pressure (initially) to control the flood of juice. The height of each cheese depends, of course, on the type of press being used, and therefore the pressure capable of being applied. Half a dozen layers of pulp is a standard quantity to press at any one go for a medium-sized press.

The cheese

This arrangement provides very good drainage channels for the juice (just as traditional setups did), which is collected in the tray or trough (made of hardwood timber, synthetic materials, or traditional stone—all materials unsusceptible to attack by apple juice) at the base of the press.

Whatever press you use, the juice will come pouring out with a distinctly muddy appearance, due to the almost immediate onset of oxidation of the tannins. This is perfectly normal, but the cider you make will be a beautiful clear golden color. Remember to taste the juice as you go along and, if possible, adjust for sweetness, acidity, and tannin by pressing more of the appropriate apples. If, however, you have only one type of apple at your disposal and you feel the balance is wrong or the juice is insipid, there are one or two additives you can use from the winemaker's cupboard to arrive at a better balance before you embark upon the fermentation discussed in Chapter 10. Obviously, this will depend on how you feel about additives in general, but it has to be said that an insipid juice will give a very poor cider, and to correct the problem at this point is much better than gross disappointment later.

Adjusting Acidity

To adjust for lack of acidity, make up a small concentrated solution of malic acid (if available), citric acid, tartaric acid, or a mixture of these in as small a volume of very hot water as possible. Now add a little of this solution to a specimen 5 quarts (4.5 liters) of juice. Shake thoroughly to distribute evenly, taste, and if necessary, add a little more acid. See how the overall quality of the juice is immediately improved, but do not overdo the acid. Make a note of the total volume of acid you added to the 5 quarts (4.5 liters), then add on a pro-rata basis to 25-30 quart (22.5-28 liter) quantities if you are working with these volumes.

To adjust for over acidity, you can use either precipitated chalk or, better still, potassium carbonate (its neutralization products leave no taste), by thoroughly dissolving a little in the juice incrementally, and once again tasting as you go. Frankly, this problem will only arise if you are endeavoring to make cider with far too high a preponderance of culinary fruit.

You may wish to be more scientific in your estimation of the juice's level of acidity by investing in an electronic pH meter. You are aiming for a juice that has a pH somewhere in the region of 3.2 to 3.8. Avoid the use of garden pH meters or pH papers or solutions that are far too inaccurate to be of any use to us here.

Balancing Tannin

To adjust for poor tannin levels, add and thoroughly dissolve a pinch of winemaker's tannin in every 5 quarts (4.5 liters) of juice, and as much as half a heaping teaspoon of tannin per 25-30 quarts (22.5-28 liters) of juice. Alternatively, you can add up to 2 tablespoons of strong tea as a source of tannin per 5 quarts (4.5 liters) of juice. Juices that make the mouth pucker severely are likely to have too much tannin in them. This can be fixed by adding a little proprietary gelatin finings. Dissolve a little of this in hot water and then add on a trial basis to establish its efficacy. The tannin will be thrown out of solution, but don't worry about filtering at this stage.

Pectolytic Enzyme

Fresh well-balanced juice made in the fall from the current crop of apples is unlikely to require the addition of a pectic or pectolytic enzyme, since it has a sufficient concentration of its own natural enzyme. If this is the case, the general advice is not to bother with this addition. Juices, however, that are derived from a high proportion of dessert apples or/and from relatively long-stored fruit will benefit from the addition of the enzyme as a preemptive strike against the possibility of haze in the final cider. Pectin is a natural carbohydrate found in all apples (and many other fruits) and, when released during fermentation, can be precipitated by the developing alcohol to produce a characteristic pectin haze. The usual recommended dosage is 2 tablespoons of the enzyme per 5 quarts (4.5 liters) of juice, making certain it is well dissolved.

Making any of these adjustments of acid, tannin, and pectolytic enzyme may very well be worth considering and are recommended if you believe the juice warrants them. You could experiment with a small amount of juice (5 quarts, 4.5 liters, or so), label the final cider clearly to distinguish it from the rest, and then determine whether the taste and character have justified the extra solicitations.

Increasing Sweetness

Any lack of sweetness in the pressed juice (and therefore the ultimate alcoholic strength of the cider) is probably best adjusted at the first racking stage as discussed in Chapter 10. This gives the opportunity for the young cider to be taken off the lees and, providing the ambient temperature is warm enough, will not slow the process down at all. However, if fermenting at much larger volumes, say, in barrels, it is recommended you adjust the sweetness at the pressed juice stage to avoid the need for an earlier racking. Add white sugar as a syrup to the juice. Make up the syrup by adding a measured weight of white sugar to a pan with the minimum of water needed to produce a clear syrup upon gentle boiling. Allow this to cool before adding.

You will first need to measure the specific gravity (SG) of the juice and then add the sugar (syrup) per 5 quarts (4.5 liters) at the rate indicated by the hydrometer to bring it to the preferred ultimate alcoholic strength. (See text sections on specific gravity and Appendix 4.) You can, of course, substitute glucose syrup, or, if you have no problems with it, apple juice concentrate as alternatives to white sugar. You will need to make your own calculations regarding strength. Alternatively, you may hold to a purist point of view and be opposed to the addition of any sweetening agent, in which case you will proceed with fermentation to make a dry cider or/and refer to Chapter 10.

Spent Pressed Apple Cake

Pomace is the term used for apple pulp either before or after juice extraction. The spent pressed apple cake should be put in a large container or plastic trash bag as you proceed. There were examples traditionally of small quantities of water being added to it and a second pressing undertaken, but in our experience, the amount and quality of the resulting juice simply doesn't justify the time or effort. The spent apple or pomace was often fed to the pigs. If you don't have a pig, however, chickens love it. If you don't have chickens, compost it, layering it between other kitchen waste and composting material.

Finally, remember after your cidermaking sessions, or each time you use the equipment, to thoroughly wash it in cold water, removing all traces of juice and milled apple. A high-pressure hose can be particularly useful. Leave the equipment to thoroughly dry, then store. When you come to it again, perhaps after a year's absence, it should, after a quick swill round with cold water or a little sterilizing fluid (rinsed off), be sweet and ready for use again.

10

FERMENTATION

Ye wolle obferve a greate agitafion at the ope of the barrelle.
Some faye yt is the werme at werke, otheres the scavengyng
beetle bringes forthe the cydere.

Once pressed, the apple juice is ready to be
fermented, and should be started without
delay. From now on, the techniques you
use will decide what kind of cider you
finally get to drink. Assuming you started
off with a balanced mix of apples, or
adjusted juice, the cider will always be
delicious, but you will have to decide what
type you prefer: still, naturally conditioned,
artificially conditioned, completely dry,
medium-dry, medium-sweet, even-sweet,
etc. All of these are possible, and this
chapter is devoted to the approaches
needed to arrive at any of the above ciders,
still or conditioned.

Recommended fermentation vessels

It is also worth mentioning that not
everyone's taste, say, within a family, is
the same. It seems a pity that for want of a little flexibility and readiness to
experiment to make different ciders, some members of the family or wider
circle are excluded from enjoying the final product.

Preparing Fermentation Vessels

If you haven't pressed the juice directly into fermenting vessels, you should transfer it either into glass demijohns or food-grade (preferably white, avoid highly colored) 25-30 quart (22.5-30 liter) plastic fermentation drums that can take a rubber bung/cork and fermentation lock. Any other suitable glass or plastic vessels can be used (e.g., old Winchesters, sherry containers, or acid carboys, provided they are strictly clean and smell sweet). Similarly, wooden vessels such as old oak casks or barrels can be used if available, but not metal barrels, with the exception of food-grade stainless steel (which can be expensive). Never use anything smelling musty. The strictures regarding cleanliness and smelling sweet apply to any vessel the apple juice or cider comes into contact with, including the bottles you may eventually use to store the finished product. Avoid any other metal container. Remember, apple juice and cider are both acidic and can easily taint.

Make certain the vessels are thoroughly clean and washed out with cold water, then use a little sterilizing fluid. Swill this around with a tiny amount of proprietary fluid, 1 or 2 Campden tablets (potassium metabisulfite) crushed and dissolved in a little water, or half a heaping teaspoon of sodium metabisulfite crystals with a pinch of citric acid in a little water. All of these exploit the toxicity of sulfur dioxide to microorganisms (and to higher forms of life in sufficient concentration). Remember, when using sterilizing chemicals, always to work in a well-ventilated area, because you are dealing with irritants.

When sterilizing, make certain that immediately afterward you rinse everything out well with cold water to remove traces of the sulfur dioxide or other chemicals, because the chemical residue might inhibit or even kill the culturing yeast used to ferment the juice in the fermentation stage.

Sulfating Before Fermentation?

One Campden tablet will provide the equivalent of 50 parts per million (ppm) of sulfur dioxide dissolved in 5 quarts (4.5 liters) of liquid. Other sources of sulfur dioxide have already been referenced.

Some cidermakers and other commentators recommend adding up to 2 Campden tablets per 5 quarts (4.5 liters) of juice prior to fermentation on the grounds of suppressing wild yeasts and bacteria in the juice, which may contribute to the possibility of spoilage. Once again, whether you follow this advice will depend on the nature of the juice you have produced and your general attitude toward additives of this kind. Two things are clear. First, purists abhor the use of sulfur dioxide and insist, with some justification, that providing the juice is fresh and well balanced, the equipment scrupulously clean, and the culturing *Saccharomyces* yeast (either natural or added immediately after the juice is pressed) is in sufficient concentration, there is simply no need ever to be involved with Campden tablets or other sources of sulfur dioxide. Secondly, it is also true that sometimes the above criteria are not met, in which case there is some evidence to suggest that adding Campden tablets to the juice can help. There can be no doubt that insipid juices, those having too little acidity (pH values above 3.8), are prone to microbial infection due to native microbes in the juice, and adding Campden tablets can inhibit their growth, while at the same time allowing a much higher concentration of existent desirable *Saccharomyces* yeasts to continue to grow. The question, nevertheless, has to be asked: why is an insipid acid-deficient juice being made in the first place?

The crux of the situation is whether the desirable *Saccharomyces* yeasts are in sufficient concentration in the juice, since sulfur dioxide is also toxic to these and not just to the undesirables. If the level of the yeasts is initially low, adding Campden tablets/sulfating at this stage could inhibit successful fermentation altogether. The point is that even if undesirable microbes in the juice have been suppressed by sulfur dioxide, unless the fermentation gets off to a galloping start, quickly leading to a blanket of "sterile" carbon dioxide above the juice, other sets of airborne yeasts and bacteria will quickly move in to spoil the juice anyway. Such is the nature of microbiology. Many cidermakers do use sulfite, particularly to destroy the wild *Brettanomyces* yeasts, found in some juices, that are held responsible for forming an unpleasant condition known as mouse taint. If you've suffered from this problem, the remedy is available in sulfite.

In twenty years of cidermaking, we have never actually had the need to use Campden tablets in the juice, but then we've always been able to follow the code below:

- Always use thoroughly washed and sound fruit, preferably recently gathered.
- Never make an insipid acid-deficient juice.
- If you do make an insipid acid-deficient juice, at the very least, as described earlier, always correct the acid imbalance before fermentation.
- Make sure the nutrient nitrogen and phosphorus levels are adequate and the juice is in a warm enough place—at least initially for the *Saccharomyces* yeast to get the fermentation underway quickly.

If you cannot follow this code for whatever reason, or if you are of a particularly nervous disposition, then sulfate with 1 Campden tablet per

5 quarts (4.5 liters) of juice. If you intend to pitch with a proprietary wine yeast as described below, however, do not do so until at least twenty-four to thirty-six hours have elapsed after having treated the juice with Campden tablets or metabisulfite. This is to allow time for the free sulfur dioxide to discharge itself by killing the low levels of spoilage organisms, thereby minimizing the chances of damaging the culturing yeast you intend to add.

Fermenting the Juice

Traditionally, nothing was added to the juice. Naturally occurring yeasts present in the air or those persisting from season to season on the equipment in the ciderhouse would simply convert the sugars in the juice into alcohol, i.e., produce the cider. It is now known that very little of the wild *Saccharomyces* (sugar fungus) yeasts responsible for fermentation actually exist within the fruit itself. Other wild yeasts do, but these are more a source of trouble than help. The obvious signs of fermentation taking place are a vigorous frothing at the mouth of the cask or barrel, usually occurring within a day or two of pressing, or a little longer if the temperature was colder. You may wish to follow this traditional method, and there are many modern cidermakers who do so successfully all the time. Indeed, they regard it as a virtue, claiming the product is superior as a consequence. These cidermakers generally adopt a laudable purist line in their craft. A word of caution, however. Nine times out of ten, apple juice, under normal circumstances, will begin to naturally ferment. But occasionally—because of low temperature, insufficient concentration of wild *Saccharomyces* yeasts or their nutrients in the juice, or for other indeterminate reasons—the fermentation is sluggish or refuses to get going. If this state of affairs continues for more than a day or two, the juice, because it will come in contact with the air, will quickly begin to spoil, turn sour, and become unusable.

For this reason, we recommended you use a fresh, good-quality, proprietary, dried wine yeast (usually varieties of *Saccharomyces cerevisiae* or *banyanus*), which has yeast nutrients added to it. These nutrients usually come in the form of ammonium phosphate, or some other source of nitrogen and phosphorus, and ensure rapid and reliable growth of the yeast. The other advantage to adding a wine yeast of this type is that it will be relatively alcohol tolerant, giving the cidermaker a greater flexibility over the final product. Baker's or brewer's yeasts should not be used.

As soon as possible after the juice has been pressed, add a couple of teaspoons of dried yeast compound to each 5-quart (4.5 liter) demijohn, swirl it around, put in a loose sterile cotton wool plug for the first few days, place the jar on a piece of newspaper, and leave it in a warm place, such as a kitchen. For 25-30 quart (22.5-28 liter) quantities of juice, 4 heaping teaspoons of yeast compound are sufficient. For even larger-volume containers, add yeast on a pro-rata basis.

A convenient plastic fermenter

Within a day or two of adding the yeast (or without, if adopting the traditional method), it should be obvious the fermentation is well under way, because of the brown debris that should be emerging from the top of the demijohn, often lifting off the loose cotton wool plug and running down onto the newspaper below. This will continue for a couple of days or so before the fermentation relaxes and settles down. At this stage, use a cotton wool swab soaked in warm water to clean the inside neck of the demijohn (and the outside) and fit a fermentation lock, which allows the carbon dioxide to escape while preventing the entry of air. Top up with cold water to replace lost juice to within about 1 in. (2-3 cm.) of the base of the bung.

From now on, leave it in a room where the temperature is about 60°F (15°C). The juice will, however, ferment at much lower temperatures than this if necessary. If you want to start drinking the final cider sooner rather than later, at Christmas or the New Year for example, you can ferment at a higher temperature, say, 70°F (21°C), but don't go beyond that range of temperature (see Chapter 12).

If you can't or don't want to fast ferment, that's fine. Providing the initial fermentation is underway and it isn't subsequently too cold, the fermentation will just proceed more slowly. It is advisable, however, not to allow the fermenting juice to ever get so cold that fermentation stops or becomes stuck, because once that happens and remains for any period of time, the possibility of the juice spoiling increases considerably. The constant production of carbon dioxide by the fermentation process keeps the juice from spoiling and makes certain you control the process.

Similarly, try to avoid sharp fluctuations in the ambient temperature, because conventional wisdom is that a smooth fermentation produces a better product. The amount of sugar in the apple juice before fermentation begins will, if entirely converted, determine the level of alcohol in the final cider. A hydrometer indicates the approximate sugar content by measuring the specific gravity (SG) of the juice. In the unfermented pressed juice, the specific gravity (sometimes referred to as the original gravity, or OG) is likely to be between 1035 and 1060, depending on the overall "sweetness" of the mix of apples you used to arrive at the juice. This table indicates the maximum alcohol potential if all the sugars are converted:

Specific Gravity (SG)	Alcohol by Volume (abv)
1035	3.7
1040	4.3
1045	5.2
1050	6.1
1055	7.0
1060	7.8
1065	8.5
1070	9.3

It can be seen that a 5-degree rise in specific gravity, attributed to sugar, results in an approximate rise in alcohol by volume of 0.6% to 0.8%, depending on the SG. If you want to know what potential alcohol could result just from the sugars in your juice, if completely converted, you will need to take a specific gravity reading before fermentation is started and consult the above table (see Appendix 4 for further discussion on the use of the hydrometer).

The yeast will continue to ferment the juice until it reaches a point at which the sugars have been exhausted or the alcohol level has risen to the limit of the tolerance of the yeast. Whichever of these two factors is arrived at earlier will determine when the fermentation ceases. It can take anywhere from two weeks to several weeks or even months for the juice to ferment out completely, depending upon the temperature and original sweetness of the juice.

When we begin to approach the end of this first stage of fermentation, it will be time to rack the cider.

Use an airlock to keep your cider from spoiling during fermentation.

Racking

Racking is the term used when siphoning off the completely or largely fermented juice from the apple lees and yeast deposit at the bottom of the fermentation vessel. It can also be used as a technique to remove the still-sweet cider from the lees before all the sugar has been consumed. It is an extremely useful and important technique that, apart from helping to stabilize and clear the cider and reduce potential off flavors from the dying yeast (autolysis), will be used as the starting point for the actual cider you want.

The point at which this first racking should take place is when the fermentation has very nearly ceased, as indicated by the extremely slow passage of bubbles through the lock and by observing that the young cider is slightly murky, with a good bed of yeast and lees. Alternatively, a hydrometer can be used. This will register a reading of about 1005 or below when the fermentation is reaching its end, indicating that almost all the sugars have been converted.

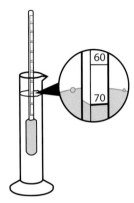

The correct reading here is 1070.

When this point is reached, siphon off the cider from the lees and yeast deposit by first tying a siphon tube 1 in. (2 cm.) or so from the end of a clean cane and inserting the arrangement down to the bottom of the fermentation vessel. Alternatively, shepherd crook siphoning devices that avoid the lees are available.

Rack into another clean vessel of a similar capacity, top up with cold water, and proceed to the next stage. If, however, you are not doing this because sugar was already added at the juice stage, go to the section "Making Different Still Ciders." If you hold a purist belief against adding sugar, go to the section "Making Medium-dry, Medium-sweet, and Sweet Ciders Using Traditional Means."

Adding Sugar

Adding sugar to the racked cider is an optional stage, though a recommended one if the juice wasn't sweetened earlier. Adding white sugar at this point will increase the alcoholic strength of the final cider and is especially useful if you started off with a juice that was low in natural sweetness.

Add granulated white sugar at the rate of about 6 oz. (170 g.) to every 5 quarts (4.5 liters) of young cider. Do this by first adding the sugar to a pan with the minimum amount of water needed to produce a syrup when the mixture is gently warmed. This quantity of sugar will increase the gravity of the cider by 15 degrees and increase the alcoholic strength by about 2.5% by volume. There is no attempt here to try to produce a cider up to the maximum alcohol tolerance of the yeast—the intention is to produce ciders of moderate strength and excellent quality. You may, however, wish to experiment in producing ciders of greater alcoholic strength. Certainly, you could easily double or triple the above amount of sugar per 5 quarts (4.5 liters), but if you do, remember you will need to know the alcohol tolerance of the yeast you are using. You should also be aware fermentation will take much longer (with the cider certainly not being ready for Christmas), and that beyond a certain point, what you will be really making is more of an apple wine.

Having added the cooled sugar syrup, top up the fermentation vessel with cold water to 1 in. (2.5 cm.) below the level of the bung with its fermentation lock and return the vessel to a temperature of 60°F (15°F) or warmer. The fermentation will again revive within a day or two of adding the sugar syrup (although it will not be as vigorous as before) and, with time, a smaller deposit of yeast will begin to settle to the bottom.

Left to continue to ferment, the cider will once again proceed to a natural dryness. The approach in this book is to do just this. If a dry cider is required, this fermented-out cider is simply bottled or stored in other suitable containers. If a medium-dry, medium-sweet, or sweet cider is desired, the approach is to ferment to dryness as above, then add further small quantities of white sugar syrup up to the desired taste, taking care to observe the procedures for storage (see below). This is an approach also used by some commercial manufacturers.

Making Still Ciders

Dry still cider

To make this cider we need to use the racked, completely fermented, young cider (whether having been through the sweetening stage or not). The appearance should be a hazy golden color and its taste very dry and slightly acidic. Bubbles through the fermentation lock should have ceased or all but ceased, and the hydrometer reading should be 1005 or below.

If the cider is unpalatably acidic at this stage, leave it in the demijohn or fermentation vessel for a month, but move it to a warmer place where a slightly different kind of fermentation, known as malolactic fermentation, can occur. This type of fermentation is brought about by a family of bacteria called *lactobacilli* (see Appendix 3), which converts the more acidic malic acid into the less acidic lactic acid. Taste the cider at regular intervals until it seems, though still unmellow, rounder and more palatable. Whether going through this malolactic fermentation stage or not (if the cider is already palatably dry), transfer the cider to as cold a place as possible under lock. If fermenting at barrel volumes, rack one further time, then leave the cider in the barrel in as cold a place as possible. When judged to be ready by taste, introduce the tap to the barrel and serve from this. Remember, however, that the cider will be in contact with a certain amount of yeast and, furthermore, how successfully the drink keeps in the barrel will depend on how quickly it is consumed (see Chapter 11). If operating at demijohn or 25-30 quart (22.5-28 liter) plastic fermenter level, over the next few weeks, the cider will clear or remain slightly hazy without ever clearing completely. This is perfectly normal for some ciders and does not affect the drinking quality. There should be no sign of activity in the cider or through the fermentation lock during this period. Rack off one last time from the small amount of yeast deposit that has formed at the bottom. Finally, add 2 Campden tablets and store the cider in any suitable containers, making certain they are filled up fully to exclude air and that the tops are on securely. Storing in screw-top bottles is a very convenient method, along with the use of corked wine bottles with a suitably designed label. Store in a cool dark place where the cider will mature over the coming months, although it is ready for consumption as it meets your taste.

Medium-dry still cider

Instead of bottling the final racked relatively clear cider above, we can now sweeten it a little with cooled white sugar syrup until it is to our taste or has an SG of about 1010. If the cider is very clear at this stage (that is, free or virtually free of yeast), it is safe to bottle it with a cork, providing it is placed in a cold shed or garage. As an added precaution, 2 Campden tablets could be added here to kill any yeast that might have been brought through. The final product, when opened, may be slightly spritzy, but will otherwise be still. If the cider is in any way cloudy or even significantly hazy, it is probably best stored in clean demijohns under a fermentation lock, or vessels with a pressure relief device. Drink it when you consider it pleasant to do so. Alternatively, the slight sweetening process of the dry cider can be undertaken just prior to drinking it.

Medium-sweet and sweet still ciders

The same procedure is adopted for both of these, adding sugar syrup to about SG 1014-1018. Once again, for safety, it is best to store these in demijohns with a lock or in vessels with a pressure relief device. Place the storage containers in a cold shed or garage. Alternatively, the sweetening process can be done on the dry cider just prior to drinking. A further alternative is the use of artificial sweeteners such as saccharin, aspartame, sorbitol, or lactose, this last being the most natural of the options. All of these are non-fermentable substances and therefore allow these sweetened ciders to be bottled if so desired.

Naturally Conditioned Ciders

A naturally conditioned cider is one in which the carbon dioxide is produced by a small secondary fermentation occurring in the bottle. Such ciders characteristically have a fizz and sparkle and are quite delicious. So-called champagne ciders are perhaps the pinnacle of this type of sparkling cider, being of the very highest quality and traditionally bottled with the typical wiring to the cork.

Champagne cider

Using a special technique known as remuage, the yeast responsible for the conditioning is also removed before wiring the champagne bottle closed. Remuage, or riddling, involves keeping the bottle inverted, twisting it daily for about a week, so the yeast is worked down onto the cork. The neck of the bottle is then plunged into an ice/salt mixture to freeze the plug of yeast, which can be ejected once the bottle is removed from the freezing mixture. The bottle is finally topped up with cider or water before re-corking and rewiring. Once again, this is not an especially difficult procedure, and you may wish to spend a little time trying it out once you have made your sparkling ciders as described below.

Normally live cider indicates there is a tiny layer of live yeast in the bottle, and that type is being referenced here. The procedures indicated in this chapter produce very high-quality conditioned ciders—dry, medium-sweet, or sweet. Sparkling naturally conditioned cider is best drunk well chilled and in smaller quantities, a bit like a fine white wine.

There are several important factors determining how quickly a bottled cider will acquire condition:

* the amount of yeast in the bottle
* the surrounding temperature
* the length of time the cider is in the bottle
* sweetness (concentration of sugar)
* the type of bottle used

If you want a delicious naturally conditioned bottled cider, but one that avoids the possibility of burst bottles due to excessive build up of carbon dioxide, it is very important to observe the following:

(1) Always make certain the yeast in the bottle is at an absolute minimum—no more than the slightest paint layer. This will be achieved by making certain the cider you are working with is racked to a haziness (only tiny amounts of suspended yeast deliberately brought through on racking) and not cloudy before bottling.

(2) Always keep the bottled cider in a cold shed or garage.

(3) Assuming observations 1 and 2 are in place, the amount of conditioning will build up with time. It can take a couple of months with so little yeast and a cold environment before a nice sparkle develops. If you want to be certain of a degree of condition before this period of time, keep the bottles in a warm (but not too warm) environment for a week before putting them in the shed. You can also increase the amount of condition a short while prior to drinking by bringing the bottle into a warm area, say for a few days, then refrigerate immediately before drinking. This stratagem should only be necessary if the cider hasn't been in the bottle long, but for various reasons, you want to drink it with a sparkle.

(4) Over time, the concentration of sweetness in the bottle will govern the amount of conditioning. Assuming the alcoholic strength of the cider is well below the alcohol tolerance of the yeast, the tiny amount of yeast in the bottle will continue to ferment the sweetness of the dissolved sugar, building up the condition continuously. This means that a bottle opened up, say, after six months will be extremely lively and with little if any remaining sweetness, because most/all of the residual sugar will have been fermented. The same bottle opened up after, say, two months, will be moderately sparkling and still relatively sweet.

(5) It is crucial that the bottles into which the cider is put are of the type that can take pressure. These include the old brown quart bottles with ceramic or plastic screw tops and rubber seals, the "clip top" type of beer bottles of various capacities, "crown corked" beer bottles, and commercial carbonated cider and soft drink bottles, usually with a metal or plastic screw cap. It is also possible to buy or collect champagne-type glass bottles and to purchase either cork or plastic tops with the wiring for these bottles. Some people have also had success, for example, with the humble plastic carbonated soft drink

bottles, and these may also be worth exploring, though be careful not to commit your whole batch to them in case of failure.

Always leave a space of 1 in. (2.5 cm.) above the cider when bottling for naturally conditioned ciders. Bottles, however, which are quite unsuitable for conditioned ciders are wine bottles or indeed any bottle that originally was not designed to take pressure.

There are other methods of temporarily storing and serving these ciders, as discussed in Chapter 11.

Dry naturally conditioned cider

To make this cider we need to use the racked completely fermented out young cider (whether having been through the sweetening stage or not). This time, a little yeast sediment should be brought through with the liquid so we are working with a cider that is slightly hazy (not cloudy). To get to this stage, you may have to rack the cider a second time. Now add white sugar syrup to the vessel equivalent of 1 heaping teaspoon of white sugar per 20 fl. oz. (591 ml.) or just less than 2 teaspoons per quart (liter). If you are using 5-quart (4.5 liter) demijohns, then add the sugar syrup, fit a rubber bung, and, while holding this, invert and shake the vessel to get the sugar completely evenly dissolved for a minute or so. If you are working with much larger volumes, add sugar syrup on a pro-rata basis and shake the vessel thoroughly to get the sugar evenly distributed. Now bottle, making certain that you leave about 1 in. (2.5 cm.) of space between the top of the cider and the top or cap. Store in a cold dark place, and referring again to the points regarding the build up of condition in the cider, this sparkling dry cider should be ready to drink within 3 months or earlier (see the methods listed previously for increasing the speed of conditioning).

Medium-sweet naturally conditioned cider

Observe the previous method, but this time, add cooled sugar syrup in small quantities to the demijohn, shaking thoroughly each time before tasting, until the cider is just sweet to the taste (about SG 1014). It is very easy to over sweeten by mistake. Remember that carbon dioxide is itself acidic, and the conditioned cider you get to drink will actually be less sweet and more acidic than at this stage. Exactly how much less sweet and more acidic will, of course, depend on how long the bottle is stored before you drink it. If you are working with much larger volume vessels, say 25-30 quart (22.5-28 liter) capacities, you will need to determine the amount of sugar syrup that is to your taste for

5 quarts (4.5 liters). Siphon off this volume into a specimen demijohn, and then add the requisite amount of sugar syrup to the remaining bulk of cider on a pro-rata basis. Make certain, having done this, to spend a few minutes shaking the vessel (or even leave overnight) to ensure the sugar is evenly dissolved throughout the whole cider. Then bottle as above and store. Given the higher concentration of sugar in this cider, the conditioning will be ready earlier than for a dry cider, but is still likely to take at least a couple of months before there is anything appreciably formed by way of a sparkle.

Sweet naturally conditioned cider

Observe the above procedure, but add sugar syrup in stages, shaking each time and tasting, until the cider is sweet (be careful not to make it sickly sweet). Having once added too much sugar, you cannot reverse it except possibly by blending it with a dry cider. As a guideline, the SG should be of the order of 1018. Bottle and store as before. Once again, the conditioning will begin to develop appreciably after a couple months.

Natural conditioning in bottles is an excellent way of producing this type of cider, and is perfectly safe, providing the above precautions are observed. It is inadvisable, however, to leave a naturally conditioned cider in a bottle much beyond six to nine months, unless the bottles are thick-walled and very strong, of the champagne-type, for example. Other options for sweetening (as already discussed for still ciders) involve the addition of such sweeteners as saccharin, aspartame, sorbitol, and lactose. If using these non-fermentable sweeteners, however, you will still need to add sugar at the rate of 1 heaping teaspoon per 20 fl. oz. (591 ml.) of cider to the bottle if you want the yeast to provide a natural condition to the cider.

Artificial Conditioning

Most commercially produced sparkling cider is artificially conditioned by pumping in a small quantity of carbon dioxide under pressure, then sealing the bottles. Today, relatively inexpensive devices are available for the small-scale cidermaker to do the same thing, if so desired, though there can be little doubt that a naturally conditioned bottled cider is a superior product.

There are advantages, however, to artificial conditioning, namely that by putting the cider into the bottle bright, i.e., completely clear, and then artificially carbonating before sealing the bottle, the possibility of excess carbon dioxide causing burst bottles is very largely removed. Effectively, the shelf life of such products is also much longer. In addition, the drinker doesn't have to wait for conditioning to take place, although he will really have needed to successively cold racked to ensure the cider is completely clear (free of yeast) before carbonating. Alternatively, the drink will have to be stabilized by pasteurization or sulfating (see Appendix 5) or be drunk within a short period.

Medium, Dry, and Sweet

Remember that any fermentation left to continue to completion will always yield up a completely dry cider. If adopting a somewhat purist line where medium-dry, medium-sweet, or sweet ciders are wanted, but where there is no wish to add white sugar at all, or any other sweetener, then there are two important techniques available to the cidermaker. These are known as cold racking and keeving. Make sure your mix of apples contains a higher proportion of dessert apples than otherwise. Aim for an SG in the region of 1055.

Cold racking

This procedure for arriving at a cider of the desired sweetness involves tasting the developing young cider when the fermentation begins to slow down somewhat and/or using the hydrometer. Seek at the level of the preferred sweetness to influence the rate and course of the fermentation by placing the developing cider in as cold a situation as possible, then by successive rackings until fermentation ceases altogether. Replace lost volume due to removal of yeast/lees each time with cold water up to the neck of the fermentation vessel. Effectively, the fermentation will have been brought to a premature end by using as low a temperature as possible, and progressively shutting off the fermentation by removal of yeast as quickly as possible with successive rackings. One to two Campden tablets per 5 quarts (4.5 liters) or proprietary arresting compounds can also be used to stop the fermentation. The SG for a medium-dry cider would be about 1012, for a medium-sweet cider about 1014, and for a sweet cider about 1018-1020. This is not a difficult procedure, but it is quite time consuming, and since you will have only fermented out a part of the natural sugars, your ultimate cider will be very weak in alcohol, unless the apples you started off with were very rich in sugar. On the other hand, it is often said that these ciders are fruitier than their sugar-sweetened counterparts.

Keeving

Keeving is an altogether more complicated process than cold racking, but is likely to be of interest especially to those cidermakers who are fascinated by these traditional techniques. The term itself probably arises from *keeve, cuve,*

or *cuvage*, all words from the French associated with
vats, casks, and fermentation. The process of keeving
is used to deliberately create a juice low in nutrient
levels. In this way, the fermentation throughout
remains slow, and, coupled with periodic
rackings, enables ciders to be produced that
have never completely fermented out. There
are similarities here, of course, with cold
racking, but keeved ciders are characteristically
brilliantly clear, lower in tannin than their
conventionally produced counterparts, and
usually quite delicious.

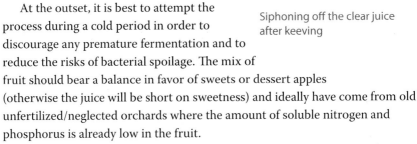

Siphoning off the clear juice
after keeving

At the outset, it is best to attempt the
process during a cold period in order to
discourage any premature fermentation and to
reduce the risks of bacterial spoilage. The mix of
fruit should bear a balance in favor of sweets or dessert apples
(otherwise the juice will be short on sweetness) and ideally have come from old
unfertilized/neglected orchards where the amount of soluble nitrogen and
phosphorus is already low in the fruit.

The pulp is made in the normal manner, but instead of being pressed
immediately is packed (not too tightly) into open-topped plastic barrels or
trashcans and left to stand for a day. This process of steeping, or maceration
(sometimes referred to as cuvage), encourages the leaching out of the pectin
and the oxidation of tannin to produce a dark brown juice that is pressed out
after the day's standing.

Over the coming week, left to its own devices, this juice will ideally separate
into a dark brown mucky head, known by the French term as *chapeau brun* (a
brown collection of lees that appears in suspension in the vessel), and a clear
golden juice that can be siphoned off. The process actually occurs because
natural enzymes in the apple juice convert pectin to pectic acid. Some of this
combines with natural calcium in the juice to form a gel that rises, along with
tannin-oxidized apple suspensions, to form the *chapeau brun*, while some of
the pectic acid combines with tannin to form a heavier product that sinks. To
encourage this process, add food-grade calcium chloride at the rate of .07 oz.
(2 g.) per 5 quarts (4.5 liters) to the initial pressed juice (traditionally, chalk and
salt were used). Keep the juice cold. If you are successful with the keeving, you
will be able to siphon off the very low-nutrient juice in between the upper and

lower solids. To witness this separating out of the juice can be remarkable, and it usually occurs quite suddenly, e.g., over the space of a few hours.

Now top up the juice with water if necessary, fit an airlock, and, adding no yeast (i.e., relying only on the natural *Saccharomyces* varieties present), wait for the fermentation to get underway. This will be very slow, but should be perceptible throughout the winter and into spring. As usual, make sure the ambient temperature for this process is low, but able to sustain the slow fermentation. The important thing is that you maintain control over the process so you are in a position to rack off a more or less stable cider at whatever SG/sweetness you want. This should be of the order of 1018-1020 for a sweet cider and something like 1014 for a medium-sweet.

If you want completely still ciders and have no objection to sulfating, add 2 Campden tablets per 5 quarts (4.5 liters) of cider, bottle without a head space, or store in bulk for consumption. If you do object to sulfating, you will need to make certain the cider you finally bottle or store is perfectly clear and stable by racking and keeping cold. Alternatively, you can pasteurize, if you have no objection (see Appendix 5). On the other hand, if you want naturally conditioned keeved ciders, don't sulfate, but do bottle with the cider slightly hazy. Leave the usual 1-in. (2.5 cm.) gap at the head. Condition will develop over the coming months.

If the keeving process has not been successful, in a few days you will notice the appearance of a creamy head on your pressed juice (instead of the dark brown debris), indicative of a normal fermentation having got underway. The juice will not clear as it should for keeving, but will grow progressively turbid as the yeast population rapidly grows. If this happens, you will simply have to let it take its course and you will end up with a conventional—though doubtless, still delicious—dry cider. You can, of course, sweeten it by whatever means if you so wish.

One final point: Because the juice is being left for as long as a week to keeve, the risk of serious infection from spoiling bacteria is a real one. It is advisable to sulfate the juice at the rate of 1 Campden tablet per 5 quarts (4.5 liters) of expressed juice once this has been obtained, and before the keeving process is underway. Do not sulfate later, as this will destroy the low concentrations of the *Saccharomyces* species that you need.

To summarize, you may wish to attempt this traditional technique, but perhaps in the first instance it would be worth experimenting with a small volume of juice to see how you get on. There can be little doubt that some of the finest ciders are produced by slow fermentation of nutrient-deficient juices, but it is also true that you will need a degree of luck.

There are certainly many dedicated small-scale cidermakers who operate this way, and these two techniques have long been traditional in making cider in France (indeed, the keeving process is sometimes referred to as the making of French cider), where regulations prohibit the addition of any artificial sweetening, including sugar. In Britain, however, there never were any such regulations and, once sugar became a cheaper commodity in the nineteenth century, the preference for sugar sweetening of a dry cider and then inducing a slow secondary fermentation in the barrel was a preferred technique because of its reliability. The result was a naturally conditioned sparkling cider with its own protective "head" of carbon dioxide, but one that would still require care and dedication on the part of the cellarman.

At the commercial level, manufacturers of cider don't go to the trouble of keeving or successive racking. They usually ferment out to dryness, then sweeten with non-fermentable saccharine or sorbitol or pasteurize and sweeten with sugar. Alternatively, they may sterilize by filtration of the yeast and suspensions and then do the above. They may reintroduce a small amount of yeast if they want a "live" cider, or pasteurize and then artificially carbonate or leave the cider still. Most of this technology today is actually available to the small-scale cidermaker, but you have to decide whether you want to go down that road. Pasteurization is considered in Appendix 5, and is undoubtedly a powerful means of stabilizing a cider with minimum fuss, allowing, for example, the retailer to be certain that none of his/her bottled product will ever be subject to bursts. However, for most cidermakers at the small-scale level, much of the technology is not necessary, and some deplore it. By an understanding of the processes involved and using the skills outlined above, we can make whatever ciders we want without using plate filters, pasteurization, artificial sweeteners, or artificial conditioning.

Fermentation in Eight Easy Steps

1. Put the vessel containing juice in a warm place if possible (kitchen is ideal) and add 2 heaping teaspoons of yeast with nutrients per 5 quarts (4.5 liters) of juice. Plug the opening loosely with clean cotton wool.

2. When the fermentation quiets (after two to three days), clean neck of vessel and fit fermentation lock.

3. Ferment to dryness (six weeks to three months depending on temperature and apple varieties) or until the cider has largely cleared and bubbles ceased (SG 1005 or less). The following stages 4 and 5 are optional.

4. Rack off. Add 6 oz. (170 g.) of white sugar as a syrup to 5 quarts (4.5 liters) of racked young cider and return to a warm place if possible.

5. Ferment to dryness as for stage 3 above.

6. Rack off and move to as cold a place as possible for two to three weeks until cider clears or very nearly so.

7. To make still cider, rack again.

    a. For dry still cider, if the cider is clear, simply bottle or barrel and leave to mature before drinking. If not clear, stabilize by either adding 2 Campden tablets per 5 quarts (4.5 liters) of cider, or pasteurize or filter.

    b. For a medium-sweet still cider, add white sugar syrup carefully to SG 1012-1015 and store the cider in a demijohn or barrel under lock until required and ready for drinking. Alternatively, store dry and sweeten just prior to consumption. If wishing to bottle, only do so after having stabilized the cider by adding 2 Campden tablets per 5 quarts (4.5 liters) or better, pasteurizing or sterile filtering.

8. To make conditioned ciders, first rack again as for Stage 7, but bring through a little yeast.

    a. For dry conditioned cider, add 4 heaping teaspoons of white sugar per 5 quarts (4.5 liters) of cider. Bottle in vessels that can take pressure. Store in a cool dark place for two to three months to allow condition to develop. Do not sulfate or pasteurize.

    b. For medium-sweet/sweet conditioned cider, add white sugar as a cooled syrup to SG 1012-1018 and bottle in vessels that can take pressure. Store in a cool dark place for two to three months to allow condition to develop. Do not sulfate or pasteurize.

sparkling CIDER

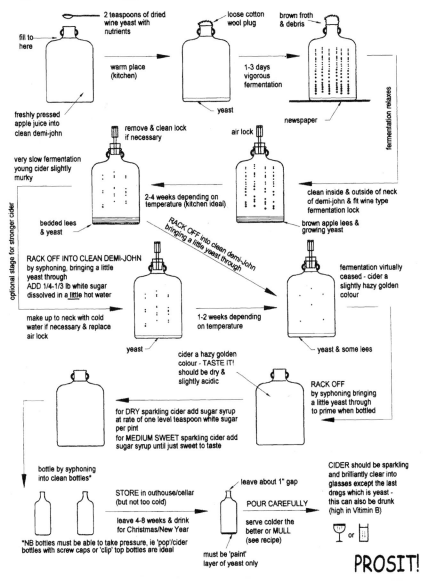

2 teaspoons of dried wine yeast with nutrients

fill to here

warm place (kitchen)

freshly pressed apple juice into clean demi-john

loose cotton wool plug

yeast

1-3 days vigorous fermentation

brown froth & debris

newspaper

air lock

fermentation relaxes

very slow fermentation young cider slightly murky

remove & clean lock if necessary

2-4 weeks depending on temperature (kitchen ideal)

bedded lees & yeast

clean inside & outside of neck of demi-john & fit wine type fermentation lock

brown apple lees & growing yeast

RACK OFF INTO CLEAN DEMI-JOHN by syphoning, bringing a little yeast through
ADD 1/4-1/3 lb white sugar dissolved in a little hot water

make up to neck with cold water if necessary & replace air lock

optional stage for stronger cider

RACK OFF into clean demi-John bringing a little yeast through

1-2 weeks depending on temperature

yeast

fermentation virtually ceased - cider a slightly hazy golden colour

yeast & some lees

cider a hazy golden colour - TASTE IT! should be dry & slightly acidic

for DRY sparkling cider add sugar syrup at rate of one level teaspoon white sugar per pint
for MEDIUM SWEET sparkling cider add sugar syrup until just sweet to taste

RACK OFF by syphoning bringing a little yeast through to prime when bottled

bottle by syphoning into clean bottles*

STORE in outhouse/cellar (but not too cold)

leave 4-8 weeks & drink for Christmas/New Year

*NB bottles must be able to take pressure, ie 'pop'/cider bottles with screw caps or 'clip' top bottles are ideal

leave about 1" gap

POUR CAREFULLY

serve colder the better or MULL (see recipe)

must be 'paint' layer of yeast only

CIDER should be sparkling and brilliantly clear into glasses except the last dregs which is yeast - this can also be drunk (high in Vitimin B)

or

PROSIT!

still CIDER

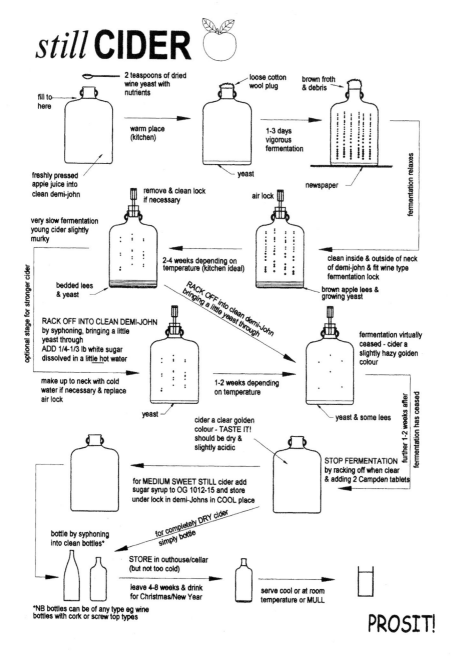

2 teaspoons of dried wine yeast with nutrients

loose cotton wool plug

brown froth & debris

fill to here

warm place (kitchen)

1-3 days vigorous fermentation

freshly pressed apple juice into clean demi-john

yeast

newspaper

fermentation relaxes

remove & clean lock if necessary

air lock

very slow fermentation young cider slightly murky

2-4 weeks depending on temperature (kitchen ideal)

RACK OFF into clean demi-john bringing a little yeast through

clean inside & outside of neck of demi-john & fit wine type fermentation lock

bedded lees & yeast

brown apple lees & growing yeast

optional stage for stronger cider

RACK OFF INTO CLEAN DEMI-JOHN by syphoning, bringing a little yeast through
ADD 1/4-1/3 lb white sugar dissolved in a little hot water

fermentation virtually ceased - cider a slightly hazy golden colour

make up to neck with cold water if necessary & replace air lock

1-2 weeks depending on temperature

yeast

yeast & some lees

further 1-2 weeks after fermentation has ceased

cider a clear golden colour - TASTE IT! should be dry & slightly acidic

STOP FERMENTATION by racking off when clear & adding 2 Campden tablets

for MEDIUM SWEET STILL cider add sugar syrup to OG 1012-15 and store under lock in demi-johns in COOL place

bottle by syphoning into clean bottles*

for completely DRY cider simply bottle

STORE in outhouse/cellar (but not too cold)

leave 4-8 weeks & drink for Christmas/New Year

serve cool or at room temperature or MULL

*NB bottles can be of any type eg wine bottles with cork or screw top types

PROSIT!

11

BLENDING, STORING, AND SERVING

*Some of the old scrumpy was so sharp and strong, you might
need two men to hold you down to drink it! I've heard it
described as strong enough to burn the name off a tombstone,
but it is probably nearer the truth to say that most farm cider
was quite weak. Given the arduous labor of haymaking and
harvest, cider quenched the thirst and replaced lost fluid,
and, more often than not, was healthier than any
water available.*

Blending is a most enjoyable art since it involves a great deal of tasting, judging,
and discussion.

Most retailed ciders—even those from small-scale cidermakers—are
blended products. This is because apart from a limited number of vintage cider
apple cultivars, such as Kingston Black or Stoke Red, most single-varietal ciders
are lacking in one respect or another and need to be blended with others to
produce a cider of character.

If you have followed the techniques developed throughout this book,
especially those concerned with establishing a balanced juice through mixing
the fruit at the outset and/or corrections to tannin,
acid, and sugar levels of the juice, there should
be little need for blending. However, if you have
access to a range of different cider cultivars, there
are advantages to pressing and fermenting single-
variety juices and then blending the final ciders to
the product you want. Seasoned cidermakers who
operate this way clearly want the control over the
processes (especially if retailing the product) that
blending ciders has over the more organic and less
systematic means of blending the fruit itself. Besides,
it is probably the only way of really getting to know

Acceptable bottles
for storing cider

the characteristics of each of the cider apple cultivars and their resultant ciders. This can be especially important as the basis of that creative dimension to cidermaking that enables customized ciders to be made.

Blending, then, is used to produce a superior cider out of individuals (either single varietals or otherwise) that are considered imbalanced or capable of improvement. The process can also be used to remedy poor ciders, but should never be thought capable of rectifying a cider smitten with problems. Gross defects sometimes occur, and you should discard such ciders without sorrow, treating their loss and your estimation of the reasons for the problems as all part of the developing experience in the craft. (Having said that, some apparently irredeemable ciders, if left for a very long time in bottle or bulk storage, have been known to miraculously resurrect themselves.)

If you intend to blend, you can do so for almost all characteristics: body, insipidity, sweetness/dryness, acidity, color, etc. The underlying principle behind blending involves bringing together ciders that are compatible, but with opposite characteristics.

Remember, if blending, to follow these rules:

- Always test your blending on a small scale first, using measured proportions, before treating the bulk.
- Be certain the ciders you intend to blend have been racked and are stable, i.e., prior to final storage, before drinking. If possible, always blend ciders of a similar age.
- Recognize that because of differences in the levels of sweetness (residual or otherwise), nutrients, acidity, and any yeast present, that blending can result in a short period of re-fermentation. As a result, you should expect to have to delay the final bulk storage or bottling for a few days until the new blended cider has re-stabilized.
- Blending may result in the appearance of hazes, sometimes after delays of various lengths.
- It is better, if possible, to blend an over-dry cider with a sweet one (and vice versa) rather than use sugar.

Storing and Dispensing

While it is true that most ciders will mature for several weeks, or even months, as their flavors stabilize and smooth out, in general the drink does not profit by any extended ageing.

There are many methods of storing, dispensing, and serving cider. Some of the options have already been touched upon, and they are further discussed here. It is really a question of what volumes of the drink are being consumed over what period. Most retailed still cider of the types being discussed, made by traditional craftsmen, should be consumed within a short period of time—a bottle on the day of opening, for example. This is because once exposed to the air, cider is apt to quickly sharpen and sour. The higher-alcohol ciders have a slightly greater protection, but still far short of a wine, which even at 11-13% alcohol will quickly sour. This problem of storage and dispensing cider dogs the retail industry, because unless a retailer has a guaranteed volume of sales, he is reluctant to take on a large quantity of cider. If it cannot be drunk quickly, it will sour in the vessel, become unpalatable, discourage both the potential convert drinker and retailer, and have to be thrown away. The net effect is to depress the interest in cider.

A storage box is the best way to keep cider for long periods of time.

The situation covering the oxidation of cider was ever thus, but at least in traditional cidermaking and drinking areas there was/is a much greater demand for the product, and an oak barrel of cider, providing it is kept in a very cool back bar or cellar or other appropriate place, can still serve up a pleasant glass months after the barrel has been broached. True, there is also the small matter of an older generation's liking or acceptance of a harsh rough cider. Today, both drinker and retailer are looking for a consistently fresh product, though one that is still a real cider.

These problems need not affect the small-scale maker and drinker of cider to anywhere near the same degree. Corked bottled dry cider probably has a good shelf life of a year and is a convenient small-volume means of consumption. Transferring dry, medium-sweet, or sweet cider from a demijohn into a jug for the social occasion is as good a way of dispensing as any, though the balance of the demijohn, even under a lock, will have to be consumed within a relatively short period of time, weeks at most. Clearly much larger volumes, such as in a barrel, can be consumed quickly if serving the needs of a party.

There is, however, another means of dispensing these still ciders from bulk, where it is possible to draw off a glass at a time and still keep the cider fresh over a period. This is a storage cube that involves an outer rigid box and an inner collapsible bag. As the cider is drawn off by means of a tap, the bag collapses, and air cannot enter to spoil the cider. This method, which has become common for wine, can be used for the amateur's cider. Such boxes can be saved, opened up, the tap mechanism removed, the collapsible bag rinsed out, and then filled again with cider. It has a shelf life of some weeks, as for wine. Alternatively, these storage boxes are available commercially relatively cheaply.

The storage box is not suitable for dispensing conditioned cider because of the presence of the carbon dioxide. Serve naturally conditioned cider chilled and straight from the bottle, or even very cold, as for a good white wine, in wine glasses or tumblers, exercising care not to disturb the tiny amount of yeast sediment. This type of cider is usually very clear if it has been left long enough in a cold environment.

12

TROUBLESHOOTING

"Oh, I've not made cider since 1939, the year they brought in rationing. We had an evacuee, a young girl from London staying with us in the country in Oxfordshire at the time. One evening, we were waiting for dinner round the table in the kitchen, when there was the most almighty explosion. Our heads went down instinctively, thinking a doodlebug (a small flying bomb used by Germany during World War II) must have hit us! After a minute, we peered up, trying to figure out the surrounding mayhem. And what had happened? A bottle of 'Ciderex' had exploded from the warmth of the range, shot upward, hit the underside of the shelf on which was set all the family crockery and sent the lot showering into pieces over the kitchen floor! I'm not sure a doodlebug wouldn't have made less mess!"

Despite good working practices—and keeping live cider by a range is not—inevitably things will go wrong from time to time. This chapter is devoted to signs, symptoms, diagnoses, and suggested remedies. It is worth saying, however, that by following the procedures and acquiring the skills established in the earlier parts of this book, you will rarely need this chapter.

Slimy Apple Pulp

Genuine cider fruit rarely causes this problem, but mixed apple pulp having a high proportion of dessert fruit can turn out to be unmanageably slimy, clogging up the press-cloths of the cheese and reducing yield considerably. The problem doesn't really affect the use of a simple basket press, because the volumes of pulp being used are much smaller and the arrangement is much simpler than with a larger press.

Changing the mix of apples with more cider or culinary varieties will certainly help by restoring the structure of the pulp, which ideally should be granular. There are also proprietary mixers available, such as rice husks, which mimic the action of the old straw in improving the drainage channels for the juice and minimizing clogging. Perhaps the best solution is to thoroughly mix in 4 tablespoons of pectolytic enzyme per 5 quarts (4.5 liters) of pulp and leave to stand overnight. The idea here is for the released pectin, which is responsible for the sliminess, to be broken down by the enzyme. This usually works well, and the resultant pulp will press well. Note that if you had intended to add pectolytic enzyme to the juice as a preventative against pectin haze, the need for this will be obviated by any additions already made to solve the problem of sliminess.

Sluggish/Failed Fermentation

It is crucial that fermentation gets underway as soon after pressing the apple juice as possible. Make certain the dried wine yeast being used is fresh or well within the date stamp on the batch. If the yeast is old or smells off, it will fail to get going and can even sour the apple juice. Be certain the wine yeast used is of a type that contains those nutrients needed by the yeast for its growth.

If you preferred to let the natural wild yeast do the fermenting, and yet, after three or four days, there seems no sign of activity (vigorous frothing at the mouth of the vessel), then you have a problem. Unless you are prepared to accept the prospect of losing the juice (or possibly as a last resort drinking it), you may have to set aside your scruples and pitch with a proprietary dried yeast compound as above. A starter bottle of yeast can always be made up prior to pitching, so that when you do so, you know the yeast is well and alive and working before going into the juice. To make a starter bottle, add a couple of teaspoons of dried yeast with nutrients and a teaspoon of white sugar to a beer bottle or similar. Now add about 3 fl. oz. (100 ml.) of tepid/warm water and swirl thoroughly. Plug loosely with sterile cotton wool and put in a warm place. Within a few hours, the yeast will be seen to have started working, as indicated by the tiny bubbles issuing from the settled yeast, causing a head or froth to appear. Swirl round thoroughly and pitch into the juice, giving this a good rousing with a sterilized wooden stick or spoon to aerate the juice thoroughly, as *Saccharomyces* yeasts need oxygen in the initial stages of their fermentation (thereafter, they function anaerobically). By such measures, with luck you may save the batch. The other major reason for a sluggish or failed fermentation is quite simply that the ambient temperature is too cold. If the fermentation is stuck, move the vessel into a distinctly warm place (such as a warm place in a kitchen). Once again, with luck the fermentation will get underway. If not, apply remedies as mentioned previously. After it has picked up, you can move the vessel back away from the warm source into a more convenient location, providing the ambient temperature is at least about 54°-60°F (12°-15°C).

Acetification

Do not confuse this with a straightforward natural acidity in your final cider (due to malic acid), which, although making an unbalanced drink and unpalatable for some people, for many is not actually unpleasant. The product is simply deemed a little harsh. Sweetening will ameliorate this acidity, but sourness due to acetification is an altogether different matter.

There are a number of routes by which cider becomes acetified, but in all of them air plays an important role in allowing the bacterium, *acetobacter*, to flourish. It is this organism that is responsible for converting the alcohol in the cider to ethanoic acid (acetic acid). This, in dilute solution, is none other than vinegar, and the cider takes on a most disagreeable vinegary taste. If the attack has been slight before identification, it is possible to neutralize the acid with potassium carbonate, but once again, prevention is much better than cure.

Unclean and unsterilized equipment is also a source of infection. However, one of the most common sources of this acetifying bacteria must be the vinegar fly or fruit fly, *Drosophila melanogaster*, which harbors the bacteria in large numbers and which, if allowed onto the apple juice or the developing cider at any time, will do its worst. Beware of it—it appears magically around any opened fermenting vessel or body of fruit juice. This is why it is important that the juice is covered or under airlock at every stage of cidermaking, the only exceptions to this being the necessary procedures for actually making the cider, such as racking, taking hydrometer readings, or bottling, all of which should be performed as efficiently as possible in terms of time and with as little aeration as possible. Remember, the juice at the outset of the process is actually at its most vulnerable to infection, because it has not yet acquired a protective head of carbon dioxide through the fermentation process.

Therefore, to minimize the chances of acetification, it is important to ensure the vessels are lightly plugged with new clean cotton wool until fermentation gets going, that the neck of the vessels are cleaned and fermentation locks fitted as soon as necessary, that the fermentation proceeds steadily, and that the young cider is then stored in such a manner (in demijohns, casks, barrels, under lock, or bottles topped up to the cork for dry ciders or with a safety gap of 1 in.,

2.5 cm., for conditioned cider) that air is excluded. When racking, transferring from one vessel to another, removing samples for hydrometer readings, etc., always make up the loss of any juice by topping up with cold water at the end of the operation to exclude air. Other reasons for souring due to acetification can be the use of yeast that is off or, in the case of bottling, by the use of inferior corks for dry ciders and faulty seals in the case of conditioned ciders, both examples allowing air in with consequent spoilage. Similarly, bottles that have been sterilized with metabisulfite solution and not rinsed out with cold water can spell death to any yeast that may be put into the bottle, say, for natural conditioning. The resulting cider will not condition, and the safety gap of air above will work on the cider to sour it.

At the end of the day, if the spoilage is just too great, you will either have to discard the product or, if you are lucky, use it in the kitchen for culinary purposes. Cider vinegar is actually wonderful stuff in this capacity, but not as a drink (certainly not in any quantity). A different sort of souring can also affect cider, some of which is also due to aerobic microorganisms. The cider is clearly off, with a very poor smell and unpleasant, even acrid, taste. This is due to a whole complex of reactions, including infection from other airborne organisms and bacterial decay of the dead yeast and apple lees. If any or all of this occurs, the resultant mess will simply have to be thrown away.

Film Yeasts (Flowers)

These wild yeasts are mostly of the *Candida* family and occur on the fruit itself and in the air. They will quickly infect any juice that is moribund in its fermentation or any improperly stored cider, especially if the yeast has already got into the juice/cider and now finds itself in contact with air.

Wash fruit thoroughly in the preparatory stages to juice making. Older fruit and damaged windfalls will need to be looked over particularly carefully. Get the fermentation off to a flying start, keep air well off the juice or developing cider, and avoid stuck fermentations. Whatever means of storing cider you are using, keep the vessels well topped up to exclude air, but remember if making a naturally conditioned cider you must preserve a 1-in. (2.5 cm.) head space.

Some people advise, as a general prophylactic to this problem, sulfating the juice before fermentation. Sulfur dioxide is certainly extremely toxic to film yeasts, but use will depend on how you feel about sulfating. Typical symptoms are a white powdery film on the surface of the cider, with heavier infestations breaking up as greasy plates that sink to the bottom of the drink. There is often an attendant sourness and taste and smell of ethyl ethanoate (ethyl acetate), which is characteristic of nail polish remover or some fruit-flavored candies. At higher concentrations, most people find this very unpleasant. Infection at this level results in the cider sadly having to be thrown away and all of the equipment and storage vessels thoroughly sterilized before any reuse. If the problem is recognized very early on with little damage, then it is best to add 2 Campden tablets per 5 quarts (4.5 liters) of juice/cider to prevent any further growth, and then set up a trial blending with good cider. You may get away with it, but don't blend in volume before having satisfied yourself it really can be saved. If in doubt, dispose of it. Bottled or otherwise stored cider that is naturally conditioning with carbon dioxide at the head will not be attacked by *Candida* film yeasts.

Cider 'Sickness'

Sweet ciders that are low in acidity occasionally suffer from this disorder. Low-acid ciders are always more prone to infection. Typically, the cider acquires a faint milky haze and rather sweet aldehyde flavors, with the drink becoming very unpalatable. The problem appears to be brought about during fermentation by a family of bacteria known as *Zymomonas*, which are involved in the partial oxidation of the developing alcohol, especially to aldehyde ethanol (formerly acetaldehyde). Little can be done but to discard the afflicted drink, not least because the implicated organisms are entirely resistant to sulfur dioxide. Once again, if the problem is caught early enough, you can try fermenting the cider out to dryness by adding nutrients and a new wine yeast culture from a starter bottle, and subsequently attempting to blend the product with good cider in the hope of ending up with an acceptable drink. As with all blending operations, however, do run it first on a trial basis, and, if in doubt, discard it.

Ropiness

So-called "ropiness" or oiliness sometimes affects ciders and wines that have been long in store. The drink pours in a thick syrup-like fashion, and although there is little alteration to the flavor, the texture is universally repellent. The condition seems to come about through a proliferation of lactic acid bacteria, which is generally welcomed, especially for the process of malolactic fermentation. However, here it is not. Vigorous stirring and/or fining/filtering to remedy or ameliorate the problem is sometimes cited, but unless this is entirely successful, the cider will need to be thrown away. Sulfating at the rate of

2 Campden tablets per 5 quarts (4.5 liters) prior to storage is usually successful as a preventative if the condition seems to afflict your cidermaking.

Mouse Taint

An offensive taint of mice, due to the formation of ethanamide (formerly acetamide), can occur in some ciders. (Although some people claim it should be thought of as an integral part of the rich array of flavors in a real cider!) Fortunately, its appearance is unusual, though seemingly capricious. It is actually due to wild yeasts of the *Brettanomyces* family along with some *lactobacilli* that have infected the apple juice and operate a minor, but damaging, fermentation parallel to the principal *Saccharomyces* fermentation to alcohol. Thorough cleaning of the apples is important. The best prophylactic is 2 Campden tablets per 5 quarts (4.5 liters) of juice (100 ppm SO_2), which should destroy this spoilage organism. Remember, do not pitch with a proprietary wine yeast until at least twenty-four to thirty-six hours have elapsed if sulfating.

If the problem appears in the cider, suggested treatments vary. The most popular seems to be the use of activated charcoal at the rate of 2 tablespoons per 5 quarts (4.5 liters) to absorb the offending chemical, followed by racking, filtering, and blending. As with all these problems, reprieve for the cider usually depends on the extent to which the problem has taken hold. Frankly, for such a problem we would recommend discarding the cider, with the usual need for scrupulous cleaning and sterilization of equipment before reuse.

Haziness

Properly made, properly managed, and stored long enough under the right circumstances, almost all ciders will turn out clear—even brilliantly clear—without the need of filtration or finings. Having said that, some ciders are reluctant to clear. It is also worth noting that people have different attitudes towards haziness in their alcoholic drinks. Today there is little tolerance, for example, for even slightly hazy beer, let alone cloudiness. By today's standards, beer should be bright. This is understandable, since cloudiness in a beer usually involves some suspended yeast and this, even if not unpleasant to taste, can interfere with, rather than add to, the flavor of the drink itself. However, often the yeast does impart an unpleasant flavor that is obviously unacceptable.

In the case of cider, the situation is both similar and different. Firstly, and most importantly, there has been a long tradition of drinking cider that quite naturally turned out somewhat cloudy or hazy. Indeed, in many quarters, the cider would almost be viewed with suspicion if it were not cloudy—at least it would prove it was real cider. This is because often, depending on the mix of apples and the circumstances of fermentation, the suspensions are either not yeast, or not largely yeast, but products of the apples themselves and therefore can be regarded as adding to the rich and complex flavors associated with real cider.

Principal amongst these natural reasons for haziness in cider is that due to pectin in the apple (this has been described earlier). There is a good case to be made for adding pectolytic enzyme to the juice before fermentation, especially if the mix of apples contains a high proportion of long-stored apples and/or dessert varieties, because it is in these that the pectin is richest and the possibility of pectin haze the greatest. Adding the enzyme to a cider that has developed the problem prior or during bulk storage, for example, may clear it, but the haze is actually caused by pectin that hasn't been broken down being thrown out of solution by the developing alcohol, so the efficacy of the treatment at this stage is much less than at the juice stage. Tannin hazes or deposits sometimes arise from the use of tannin-rich fruit, such as a preponderance of bittersweet apples in the mix. Too high a concentration of tannin in solution can mean that upon cooling, such as refrigeration prior to drinking, the tannin is precipitated out of solution as a haze. This is particularly annoying if the cider has been bottled perfectly clear. Since tannin is a significant part of the character of a cider, the object must be to retain a balance of this, but it has to be said that under normal circumstances you would be very unlucky to find yourself so afflicted with this problem. Sometimes the haziness is due to suspended yeast, sometimes working its way into a colloidal state that may prove very difficult to clear. There is some evidence to suggest that pure strains of proprietary wine yeasts bed down better than reliance on wild yeasts to perform the fermentation.

Opalescence in the cider will almost always result from an unwelcome formation of ethyl ethanoate (ethyl acetate), producing the smell of nail polish remover because of *Candida* yeasts (film yeasts as discussed earlier) or for chemical or other biochemical reasons (see below).

At the end of the day, however, most ciders will clear or almost clear naturally, especially if they are put in a cold enough environment. In the case of naturally conditioned (carbonated) bottled ciders, it is important that the cider is bottled in a slightly hazy state due to a small amount of suspended yeast necessary for the conditioning process. Over the storage months, this beds down as a "paint layer" on the bottom and, of course, produces a natural sparkle to the cider.

If you are trying to produce ciders that are always perfectly or brilliantly clear, you may very well wish to experiment with the kind of range of proprietary finings available, or any of the filtration devices.

Finings of whatever type (and there are many) exploit the fact that hazes are caused by materials with electrically charged particles of one polarity, while the choice of fining comprises electrically charged particles of an opposite polarity. The net effect is an electrical neutralization reaction in which the haze material hopefully is thrown out of solution as a suspension and the resultant cider, after filtration, ends up beautifully clear.

Two of the most widely used finings are gelatin and bentonite. This latter is particularly versatile and well regarded in winemaking circles. It is a montmorillonite clay ($Al_2O_3 4SiO_2H_2O$), widely available, and is especially good for ridding ciders of protein hazes and cloudiness. It needs to be added as a suspension in water at a dosage recommended by the manufacturers, but can actually be added to the juice as a powder at the outset of fermentation and is reputed to lead to miraculously clear ciders, leaving behind a well-compacted sediment, ready for racking off. As with all these things, it is best to perform trials, using a number of different fining preparations to establish efficacies and dosages particular to each problem.

There can be no doubt that clearing a stubbornly hazy/cloudy cider with one of these products can give you great satisfaction—especially if you feel you have reprieved a product you thought lost—but in general, there is a sneaking feeling that having to resort to filters and finings and so forth is, at the end of the day, something of a confession of failure.

Flat/Unconditioned Cider

This could be due to bottles that have not been thoroughly rinsed of a sterilizing solution. Faulty seals or chipped glass tops on the bottles are another source of lack of condition. Check these before bottling and discard any that are dubious. Similarly, bottling in an inappropriate bottle, i.e., one that is not designed to take pressure, will not produce any condition.

A cider may appear to come out of its bottle without the expected fizz and sparkle for the simple reason that it hasn't been in the bottle long enough. As we noted in the section on natural conditioning, this process depends on a number of factors including the temperature,

Ideal bottle types for naturally conditioned cider

quantity of yeast, and length of time in the bottle. Do not, however, in order to speed up the conditioning, increase the quantity of yeast beyond a paint layer, or the ambient temperature beyond cool or cold. If you do, you could end up with burst bottles.

Burst Bottles

These are due to any or all of the following: too much yeast, too warm a temperature, too high a concentration of sugar, too great a length of time in the bottle, too thin-walled a bottle, or failure to leave a 1-in. (2.5 cm.) gap at the top of the cider. Follow the strictures in the section on natural conditioning and you will never have any problems. Always store in the dark in a garage or shed. Don't bottle up cider for conditioning unless you intend to drink it within a reasonable period of time. The worst thing you can do is to bottle it up and then leave it in a shed or garage and forget about it.

If you suspect you may have too much yeast after it has bedded down, then it is better to open up and re-bottle. There will be no loss of quality. If you suspect the temperature, say in summer, to be too warm, then move the bottles to a colder place. Above all, cautiously test one or two bottles after a few weeks/months to gauge the amount of condition. If you get deluged in the fountain, then there is far too much condition and you should release the pressure carefully on all of the bottles. Drink up quickly thereafter, or repeat the pressure release operation.

Chemical Taste

This is a rare, but usually terminal problem, when it occurs. The resulting cider is usually quite unpalatable and will need to be thrown away. The active flavoring ingredient in some fruit candies is an ester called ethyl ethanoate (formerly called ethyl acetate). This naturally occurring non-poisonous chemical is found in pears and a number of other fruits, including many varieties of apple, though in very small amounts. In the fruit, it has a pleasant taste. However, it can be produced in cider at unacceptable levels (often along with small amounts of other esters) and impart a most unpleasant flavor to the drink.

It appears to come about by the reaction between the alcohol and ethanoic acid (acetic) from the partial oxidation product of some of the alcohol under the right conditions. These reactions may be partially microbiological in origin, as alluded to earlier in the case of *Candida* film yeasts. There are two principal situations that, either separately or together, will lead to this problem. If the cider is fermented at too high a temperature (for example, right up close to a radiator, or constantly near to an open fire, or some other excessive source of warmth), the possibility of producing ethyl ethanoate increases. It is permissible to ferment at higher temperatures up to 70°F (21°C), but beyond this the possibility of the above reaction increases considerably. The other reason, almost certainly compounded by higher temperatures, is when the fermentation goes on so long in contact with a large settled mass of apple lees. Some pressed juices are very thick and produce, as the fermentation gets underway, a large settled mass of brown lees. If the juice is particularly sweet, the fermentation at this stage can continue for a long time in contact with these lees, increasing the risk of the undesirable ester. The answer is to rack off at a much earlier stage.

Thus, when the fermentation has slackened off and the lees have distinctly settled down (they may be flocculent), rack off from these, top up with cold water, and continue the fermentation to dryness. Now rack off again (that is, to the first racking stage as discussed in Chapter 10), and add the white sugar syrup to the young cider, and proceed as normal. Effectively, you have introduced an earlier racking stage to remove the body of the fermenting cider from an excess of lees.

You may, on drinking a glass of real cider, detect a very slight sense of ethyl ethanoate. At this concentration, it is quite likely to be pleasant and to add to the overall cocktail of flavors that comprise a real cider.

13

DRINKS AND RECIPES

Apart from the pleasure of drinking the cider in its own right, there are many drinks to be made from it. Those given below are just a sample, all of them particularly delicious because the cider is homemade and fresh.

Drinks

WINTER'S DELIGHT MULLED CIDER

This is a delicious drink for a cold winter's night. Make sure you've been out in the cold beforehand or, if preparing it for a party, that guests arrive as thoroughly chilled to the bone as possible!

Ingredients:

For approximately 1 quart (1 liter) of fresh cider use:

* 12 whole cloves
* 1 stick of cinnamon
* 12 white/green cardamom seeds
* Pinch of grated nutmeg

Method:

Choose a suitable mulling vessel—avoid aluminum or non-stick, but a glass or ordinary stainless steel pan is suitable. A stainless steel pot of 2-3 quart (2-3 liter) capacity is ideal.

Gently simmer the cider with the spices for 20 minutes or so. Dissolve a little white sugar into the mulled cider according to preferred taste and serve hot in a tumbler or wine glass.

For a drink with a slightly bigger kick, add a measure of light or dark rum to each glass beforehand.

SUMMER CIDER PUNCH

For those glorious hot summer days, try this recipe.

Ingredients:

- 1 quart (1 liter) very cold cider
- 1 quart (1 liter) cold lemonade or soda water
- Cut-up peeled rind of an un-waxed lemon
- Juice of half a lemon
- 1 measure of whisky
- 1 measure of gin
- A little superfine sugar to sweeten to preferred taste

Method:

Combine all the ingredients in a large bowl and enjoy. As variants upon this, replace the lemon peel with pieces of orange, cucumber, mint, or other similar fruits or herbs.

HOT CIDER TODDY

Use this for colds or just as a nice drink.

Ingredients:

- 8 fl. oz. (237 ml.) cider
- 2 cloves
- A little crudely chopped root ginger
- Twist of lemon juice
- 1 tablespoon honey

Method:

Simmer the cider in a stainless steel or enameled pan with the cloves, ginger, and lemon juice for 1 minute. Strain off into a glass and add the honey.

Recipes Using Cider

Cider has long been used in recipes associated with pork, creating wonderful dishes. In fact, cider is especially good with any light meat—chicken, rabbit, and even fish.

PORK WITH CIDER AND CREAM

Serves 4

Preparation and cooking time 45 minutes or less.

Ingredients:

* 8 fl. oz. (237 ml.) dry cider
* 4 pork chops or steaks
* 1 medium-sized onion
* 2 oz. (57 g.) mushrooms
* 2 tablespoons plain flour
* Salt and pepper
* 2 oz. (57 g.) butter
* 5 fl. oz. (150 ml.) light cream
* 1 tablespoon chopped parsley
* 1 tablespoon chopped chives

Method:

Chop the onion finely. In a deep frying pan, melt the butter and fry the onion until golden. Season the flour and use half to coat the pork. Fry these lightly until brown on each side and then remove.

Chop the mushrooms and fry lightly, mixing in with the onion. Turn down to a very low heat, stir in the remaining seasoned flour to make a basic roux with the butter, and then gradually add the cider, stirring all the while. Bring to the boil for a minute. Season with a little salt and pepper, return the pork to the pan, and cover and simmer on a low heat for 20 minutes or until the pork is tender.

Now stir in the cream and chopped chives. Serve with boiled new potatoes and green or french beans.

CHICKEN OR RABBIT WITH CIDER

As a variant on the above pork recipe, try using chicken breasts or legs or similar joints from a rabbit. The onion can be replaced with several fat cloves of garlic, which should be very lightly fried and then removed. Add and mash in once the cider sauce has been made.

Fish in Cider

Serves 4

Preparation and cooking time 40 minutes or less.

Ingredients:

+ 8 fl. oz. (237 ml.)
+ 4 white fish steaks or fillets
+ 1 oz. (28 g.) butter
+ Salt and pepper
+ Juice of half a lemon
+ 1 beef tomato
+ 2 oz. (57 g.) mushrooms
+ 1 oz. (28 g.) plain flour
+ 1 tablespoon chopped parsley

Method:

Put the fish in a greased baking dish and top with sliced tomatoes and mushrooms. Season with salt and pepper, add lemon juice, and pour in the cider. Cover the dish with a lid or foil and bake in a moderately hot oven for about 20-25 minutes (or microwave for 8 minutes).

Drain the liquid off the fish, keeping this hot. Melt the butter gently in a heavy saucepan and stir in the flour to make a basic roux. Now add in the reserved cider/fish liquid to make the sauce, stirring all the while and bringing to the boil for 1 minute.

Pour the sauce over the fish and garnish with the chopped parsley. Serve with mashed or boiled potatoes and preferred vegetables.

HEREFORD CIDER SAUCE WITH BOILED BACON OR HAM

This is another delicious cider recipe, very quickly made.

Ingredients:

- 17 fl. oz. (½ liter) cider
- 1 boiling bacon or ham
- 2-3 tablespoons pork or lamb drippings
- 1 oz. (28 g.) plain flour
- 10 fl. oz. (300 ml.) vegetable or meat stock
- 2 cloves
- 1 bay leaf
- Salt and pepper

Method:

Cook the boiling bacon or ham. Melt the pork or lamb drippings in a heavy saucepan and stir in the flour to make a smooth dark roux. Add the vegetable or meat stock, stirring all the while, and bring to the boil to thicken the sauce. Now add the cider, cloves, bay leaf, and seasonings. Mix thoroughly. Pour the sauce over the bacon or ham and serve with preferred vegetables.

14

PRESERVING PURE
APPLE JUICE

The apple juice we press doesn't have to be fermented to cider—it can simply be drunk, and is so much more delicious than any commercial product you could ever buy. It really is a case of tasting is believing. Even if you have little interest in cider, but have apples and like apple juice, then owning or making a press is a must.

Once again, this pressing of the apple juice could take place at a small-scale, multi-family, or community level, where the labor and the juice are shared out among the participants. The best type of juice for drinking is sweet, but still has a nice acid dimension, as well as all the other subtle flavors. Anywhere between 60-70% sweet dessert apples with the balance of the cooker type will produce an excellent juice. However, make certain all the fruit is sound and that all apples that are moldy or have been in contact with moldy apples are discarded without compromise. Cut out the worst of internal rot and bruising (see Appendix 6).

Freshly pressed apple juice can be drunk for up to four to five days after pressing, providing the juice is kept in a refrigerator. Any amount that is not going to be drunk within this period has to be preserved within a few hours of pressing if the full flavor is to be kept and you want to drink it over the months after making. It is not a question of simply putting it in a cupboard somewhere and taking what you want, when you want. Juice left in this manner will have begun to ferment long before you have finished a fraction of it, and in a closed vessel would run the risk of explosion.

There are two basic methods of preserving the apple juice. Both are excellent. What is more, neither one involves the use of preservatives or any additives, so you know the juice is pure.

Freezing

By far the most convenient vessels to use for freezing are empty plastic drink bottles of about 1-quart (1 liter) capacity or larger.

Do not, under any circumstances, freeze the juice in glass bottles. No matter what vessel you choose to freeze the juice in, you must remember to leave a 2-in. (5 cm.) space at the top of the juice to allow for expansion upon freezing.

The advantage of this method is that it is quick, convenient, and produces juice upon thawing even months later that is as delicious as when it came out of the press. The disadvantage of the method is that it can use up a lot of freezer space and you have to remember to take it out beforehand to allow time for thawing. Once thawed, consume within four or five days at most, providing it is kept in a refrigerator.

Pasteurization

Pasteurization is a technique that kills the microorganisms (including the wild yeast) in the apple juice that bring about fermentations. Once pasteurized, the juice can be kept in bottles indefinitely and is immediately available for drinking, unlike frozen juice. The process does, however, involve a little investment of time and care to do it properly and does alter the flavor of the juice very slightly.

Clean glass bottles are needed, either the quart bottles with ceramic or plastic tops or glass soda bottles with metal tops. Other similar types of bottles, such as clip-top beer bottles, can also be used. Make sure that all seals and tops are in good condition and sterilized with boiling water, otherwise the juice will spoil.

The bottles are filled to within 1 in. (2.5 cm.) of the top with juice and then placed in a hot water bath that has been heated and held at 158°C (70°C). The water in the bath must immerse as much of the bottles as possible so all of the juice is subjected to a temperature of 158°C (70°C). Do not put too many bottles into the bath at any one time, since you need to establish a good water/heat circulation. The juice in the bottles must be held at this temperature—use a standard thermometer to keep track of temperature— for thirty minutes. Confirm that the juice in the bottles has indeed been subjected to this temperature for this period by carefully lowering the (cleaned) thermometer into the juice in one of the bottles two-thirds of the way down.

If you have remembered to leave some space at the top of the bottles, there will be no running over. If a little does, however, do not worry. At the end of the thirty minutes, remove the bottles carefully, screw on or down the caps, and place the bottles on their sides away from each other. As they cool down, a sterile vacuum seal will be created inside each bottle. Wipe the outside of the bottles free of any stickiness and store in a cool dark place. Use when wanted. Once opened, the juice will keep well for four to five days in a refrigerator. A thermostatically controlled pasteurizer can be purchased, making the job much easier, and certainly the relatively modest outlay would be justified if you have large quantities of juice. Alternatively, both the cost and usage of the device could be shared out among a number of people—another opportunity for communal enterprise (and a little party).

15

MAKING CIDER VINEGAR

Cider vinegar, as any chef will testify, is a valued culinary commodity. Some regard it as possibly superior to wine vinegar in the making of vinaigrette, and it is excellent in marinades. It is also reputed to have wide-ranging health benefits when taken in various recipes and/or as part of a daily diet.

From Dry Cider

Vinegar is a dilute solution of ethanoic (acetic) acid—on average about 5%—that comes about by the oxidation of the alcohol in the fermented product.

Making cider vinegar is a simple if somewhat lengthy process at a domestic level, because it uses the relatively inefficient Orleans process (but it is perfect for our purposes). The cider you begin with needs to be relatively strong in the first place, say 8% to 9% alcohol, because this process will only give you a vinegar at about 5% acid level. It is important for pickling purposes to have the vinegar at this degree of ethanoic (acetic) acid, because below that level there is a risk of microbial spoilage of the preserved food. On the other hand, cider vinegar is not usually used for pickling, and if you intend to use the vinegar for marinades, vinaigrette, for drinking, or as part of a diet, it is perfectly possible to start with a much weaker cider and turn it into a cider vinegar having an acid level below the accepted level of 5%.

There are two approaches. Ferment the natural juice out completely to dry cider, having racked off from the bulk of the settled lees when the fermentation begins to slow down. Add sugar as recommended at the first racked stage, unless you started with a particularly sweet juice. Rack again when the cider is once again dry and clear (or slightly hazy) and then pour it into a vessel—barrel, plastic fermenter, demijohn—up to two-thirds, leaving a good head of air above the cider. Lay the barrel on its side, if possible, to maximize the surface area of cider to air in order to promote the oxidation. If you can't lay it on its side, don't worry. Note: the cider should not be sulfated, nor should it have been sulfated in any way prior to this point, because it would inhibit the acetifying bacteria. Now put a loose mesh cloth, scrim, or muslin across the mouth of the vessel

to allow air free access (do not plug). Leave in a distinctly warm place over the coming weeks and months.

This process may be sped up by buying a culture known as a vinegar mother from an obliging small producer of vinegar. This is a gelatinous material of the *acetobacter* responsible for the acetification process. It used to be common in buying what was then unpasteurized malt, wine, or cider vinegar to see the vinegar mother floating about in the bottom of the bottle. The bacteria are also found in any hazy vinegar you may come across. In either case, introduce the culture (the vinegar mother or the hazy vinegar) to the body of the cider and leave once again in a warm place.

If you cannot get vinegar mother or any hazy vinegar, then try culturing your own acetifying bacteria by exposing an open jar of dry unsulfated cider to the air for several weeks. Smell and taste this at intervals to identify the unmistakable vinegary quality that forms because of the wild bacteria in the air, and then use this to culture the main body of cider as described above.

The idea from now on is to expose the cider to as much air as possible for two or three months, or longer if necessary. The alcohol will be oxidized by the *acetobacter*, which proliferates in the presence of air and forms the ethanoic (acetic) acid to produce the cider vinegar. Smell and taste the developing product from time to time to gauge how the vinegar is forming. When it tastes nicely vinegary and doesn't seem to be getting any more so, bottle either into corked wine bottles or screw-top bottles and store. (As an added precaution against any possibility of later fermentation in the bottle due to residual sugars and yeasts in the vinegar, you may wish to pasteurize your vinegar. Adopt the same procedures for juice preservation or cider pasteurization.)

Remember, never use the same vessels and equipment for making vinegar as you use for making cider. Keep cidermaking and vinegar making separate, and try not to perform them even physically close together, because you will want to prevent any possibility of acetification of your cider.

Making cider vinegar with the Orleans process using a glass demijohn

Appendix 1:

GLOSSARY OF TERMS

Alcohol by volume (abv): Measure of the alcoholic content of a beverage, usually expressed as the percentage (%) of alcohol by volume.

Acetification: Process by which some or all of the formed alcohol is oxidized to ethanoic (acetic) acid, which gives the cider a sharp vinegary taste.

Acidity: The sharpness in the juice or cider, measured quantitatively by pH. This is a crucial characteristic to acquire at the correct level for a good cider.

Aerobic fermentation: Fermentation by yeast or other organisms requiring air.

Ammonium phosphate: Nutrient for yeast supplying vital nitrogen (N) and phosphorus (P).

Anaerobic fermentation: Fermentation by yeast or other organisms that occurs in the absence of air.

Aspartame: Commonly used artificial sweetener in the food industry; sometimes used by cidermakers because it is non-fermentable.

Autolysis: Breaking open of dead yeast cells (which then become prone to bacterial decay and potential spoilage of cider if left on the yeast lees).

Bentonite: Diatomaceous clay used as a very effective fining.

Bittersharp: Class of cider apple reflecting the balance of tannin to acid.

Bittersweet: Class of cider apple reflecting the balance of tannin to sugar.

Campden tablets: Convenient form of sulfating with potassium metabisulfite to give the equivalent of 50 parts per million (ppm) of sulfur dioxide to 5 quarts (4.5 liters) of juice or cider; used for sterilization or stabilization of cider.

Carbon dioxide: One of the principal fermentation products; colorless, odorless, non-toxic gas that also provides condition for cider.

Cheese: Built-up pack comprising of layers of apple pulp wrapped in cloths, each layer separated by wooden or plastic racks. The whole is then pressed to release the juice.

Citric acid: Principal acid of citrus fruit; sometimes used in cidermaking to adjust acid levels; also used in conjunction with sodium/potassium metabisulfite to release free sulfur dioxide for effective sterilization.

Condition: Term used to describe drinks that have acquired (by a secondary fermentation) small amounts of dissolved carbon dioxide, i.e., a pleasant sparkle that also brings out the aromas of a drink.

Cuvage: A form of steeping or maceration in which apple pulp is left in open-topped barrels in the cold for a day to promote juice formation and induce enzymatic changes prior to the processes of pressing and keeving.

Demijohn: Common name for a 5-quart (4.5 liter) glass fermentation jar.

Dry: In the context of cider, the term describes a drink formed by the complete or near-complete fermentation of all sugars, i.e., with a specific gravity (SG) between 1000 and 1005; completely unsweet.

Enzymes: Naturally occurring (or synthetically prepared) protein catalysts that are responsible for almost all changes in brewing (and every other living process). These are the critical biological substances, for example, that yeasts use to convert sugars to alcohol.

Ethanol alcohol (ethyl alcohol): This is the main product formed from sugars by yeast during fermentation.

Fermentation: Conversion of sugars to alcohol, carbon dioxide, and water by yeasts or other microorganisms.

Filtration: Clarifying hazy or cloudy ciders using filters comprising of powders, papers, or pads.

Fining: Removal (by depositing out) of fine suspended solids that are responsible for hazes and cloudiness in some ciders. This process is brought about by the addition of finings drawn from a whole range of different sources (often animal or vegetable in origin).

Gelatin: An effective and commonly used fining.

Hydrometer: An instrument used for measuring the specific gravity (SG) of a juice, or a developing or completely fermented out drink. The instrument gives a measure of the dissolved sugar in the liquid. Usually two types: brewer's and winemaker's, the latter being used in cidermaking.

Keeving: Technique used in traditional cidermaking where enzymatic changes in apple juice are promoted to arrive at a clear low-nutrient juice that can be very slowly fermented to naturally sweet ciders. The technique is often associated with French cidermaking, where the addition of sugar or other sweeteners is proscribed.

Lactose: The principal sugar found in milk; can be obtained from brewing suppliers for use as a means of artificially sweetening ciders; has the advantage of being un-fermentable by *Saccharomyces* yeasts.

Lees: The solid deposits of fruit and/or yeast settling to the bottom of a vessel during and after fermentation.

Malic acid: The principal acid found in apples.

Malolactic fermentation: Slow lactobacillus (not yeasts) induced fermentation of ciders (and wines) that, in warmer conditions, can convert the harsher malic acid in a cider to the softer lactic acid, thereby producing a more mature, more palatable drink.

Metabisulfite: Commonly used term for sodium or potassium metabisulfite, used as the most common forms of sterilizing vessels and stabilizing ciders. The substances release sulfur dioxide in the vessel of drink, killing unwanted microorganisms.

Mock: Another term for a cheese, but one in which the apple pulp is bound up with straw instead of wrapped in polyester cloths and separated by racks; obsolete or near obsolete practice now.

Naturally conditioned: An alcoholic beverage that has acquired carbonation or a sparkle by a natural secondary fermentation occurring in the storage vessel.

Oxidation: Particular type of chemical or biochemical reaction, often requiring the presence of oxygen in air, facilitated by enzymes of microorganisms or other chemical agents. For example, the rapid coloration of apple juice once formed is due to the onset of oxidation of tannin in the juice. The acetification of the alcohol (ethanol) to vinegar (ethanoic acid) is another oxidation, sometimes chemical, sometimes biochemical in origin.

Pasteurization: A technique of holding liquids at 162°F (72°C) for a while in order to preserve them. Discovered by Louis Pasteur (1822–1895). At this temperature, the flavor of a beverage (e.g., apple juice or cider) is not demonstrably affected, but most of the microorganisms responsible for spoilage are killed. Providing a sterile vacuum seal is created above the drink, it will keep indefinitely.

Patulin: Name given to a complex of toxins created by moldy or decaying apples (and other fruit). Such fruit should never be used in making apple juice. Now believed to be destroyed during fermentation processes.

Pectin: Natural carbohydrate found in apples (and many other fruits) responsible for helping jam set and, annoyingly, the formation of a number of hazes in cider.

Pectolytic enzyme: Usually available as the synthetically prepared or extracted enzyme of that naturally occurring in apples. Pectin hazes (see above) are not that common, but can occur under the right circumstances. The addition of synthetic pectolytic enzyme at the outset of fermentation can often forestall the chance of hazes.

Press cloth: Squares of terylene, nylon, or other polyester used to wrap up the apple pulp (e.g., when making the cheese or pack) prior to pressing.

Racking: Siphoning of the cider from the lees when the fermentation has finished, or all but finished, in order to clear and stabilize the final product during storage.

Remuage: From the French meaning to move or twist; used in making so-called champagne cider. This is the technique used to work the yeast down onto the cork of the inverted bottle, prior to freezing and the removal of this sediment plug.

Riddling: See *Remuage.*

Scratter: Type of mill (hand or power-operated) with interlocking teeth that converts the apples into a fine-grained milled state prior to pressing.

Sorbitol: Artificial non-fermentable sweetener.

Specific gravity (SG): Gives a quantitative measure of the amount of sugar present in a juice or beverage. Other dissolved materials all contribute to the overall measured SG value, but sugar is by far and away the principal contributor. Knowing the SG values of starting juice and fermented product enables the cidermaker to calculate how much alcohol is present or how much more sugar to add for a desired strength.

Still: In the context of cider, the term refers to a lack of any form of carbonation in the drink, i.e., it has no sparkle.

Storage cube: Simple bag-in-a-box means of dispensing wine or cider, preventing the ingress of air to acetify the drink. Cider kept in a storage cube can be drawn off when it is wanted over several weeks without the risk of spoilage.

Sulfating: General term used whenever a juice or cider is subject to treatment by a source of sulfur dioxide, i.e., the addition of sodium/potassium metabisulfite, Campden tablets, or free sulfur dioxide for purposes of sterilization or stabilization.

Taint: Spoilage of cider by picking up trace flavors, usually from unclean, inappropriate, or outlawed vessels.

Tannin: A substance present in apples (and other fruit and many plants) that confers an important astringency to the cider. Crab apples and cider apples have good levels of tannin and it is crucial to get the correct balance of tannin for a good cider.

Ullage: This is the difference between the volume capacity of the vessel, e.g., a cask, and the actual volume of cider (or beer or wine) in the cask. In other words, it is the space above the level of the cider in a storage vessel.

Vinegar: Approximately 5% solution of ethanoic (acetic) acid formed by the bacterial oxidation of the alcohol in the cider or wine.

Yeast: Generally taken as the microorganism *Saccharomyces* (sugar fungus) responsible for fermentation, i.e., the conversion of sugar to alcohol, water, and carbon dioxide in the making of alcoholic beverages. There are many yeasts, some of them spoilage organisms.

Appendix 2
MAKING PERRY

Perry from pears is not as well known as cider, but is a distinctive drink much prized among its many followers. Especially for the small producer and retailer, cider and perry usually go hand in hand. Making perry follows exactly the same principles as those for cidermaking, although it is difficult to make good perry without using genuine perry pear varieties. There are many fine examples of these with wonderful names such as Malvern Hills, Green Horse, Tumper, Merrylegs, and Dumbleton Huffcap. Butt is another very commonly used perry pear variety. Such fruit is not recognized as a dessert pear, but contains a balance of flavors and high proportions of tannins, making a fine end product. Unlike apples, perry pears (indeed all pears) ripen much earlier, and few have any keeping properties. It is important once they are harvested to press them immediately and to get the fermentation underway.

If you would like to try making perry, but have only a selection of fruit that is of a dessert type rather than actually perry pears, then don't despair of making the drink, but recognize at the outset the inadequacies of the juice such fruit will produce and adjust this before fermentation. The fruit will be very juicy, sweet, and contain the usual selection of esters, but upon tasting, it will be quite remarkably bland and insipid, and if fermented, would produce a completely undistinguished product. Therefore, adjust for acid and tannin by the addition of these (as indicated in Chapter 9) and you are much more likely to end up with a product to your liking.

If you feel the sweetness is lacking also, then add white sugar as a syrup as indicated for adjusting apple juice in Chapter 10 (or use the cold racking technique if you are opposed to the addition of sweeteners), either before fermentation or after the first racking stage. In our experience also, perry made from dessert pears experiences more difficulty in clearing than cider, and because of this, it is advisable to add a pectolytic enzyme at the rate of 2 tablespoons per 5 quarts (4.5 liters) of juice to facilitate clarification. To some extent, this clearing problem is a reflection of overripe fruit, but you will be extremely fortunate if you can prepare your juice from fruit that has been caught just at the right point.

Naturally, if you have access to genuine perry pear varieties, you should be able to make excellent examples of the drink, but in general the best perries are of the single-varietal types, because pears do not blend well.

Perries are more conventionally produced sweet or medium-sweet (rarely ever dry), because many varieties contain significant natural levels of non-fermentable sorbitol. They are also quite often naturally conditioned in the bottle (or artificially carbonated). Follow the procedures for producing these types of drinks as indicated for those corresponding ciders in Chapter 10.

And what of pear and apple trees? The pear tree has a lovely upward curving crown whose display of blossom is a very distinctive feature of the Herefordshire and Worcestershire landscapes in Britain—a blossom that is out in all its finery weeks before that of the apple. While the perry pear tree can take many years to come into fruit, you can still find examples bearing in abundance two or even three hundred years later, when the apple tree has long been dead.

Appendix 3:

MALOLACTIC FERMENTATION

This minor fermentation is usually a welcome prospect to any cidermaker or winemaker. It can either occur in the bulk racked-off cider if left for any period of time, or in the bottle in the case of still ciders. It is usually welcome, because the fermentation alters the sharp acidity of the predominant malic acid from the apples to the less acidic lactic acid, creating a rounder smoother character to the cider. A cider already low in acidity can, if malolactic fermentation goes on too long, turn insipid, but that is an unusual outcome.

Malolactic fermentation is brought about not by yeasts, but by species of *lactobacillus* bacteria (of the types cultured in yogurt making), and apart from its smoothing effect, it can also leave an otherwise still cider slightly spritzy with the carbon dioxide given off, so that there is a general enlivening and freshening effect upon the drink.

Very often malolactic fermentation takes place quietly and inconspicuously in the spring when the weather warms up a little and the bacterial population has grown sufficiently for the change to take place. It is rare for there to be any visible sign of bacterial deposit because of the size of the microorganism. The drink remains clear throughout.

Having said all of this, malolactic fermentation is by no means guaranteed to occur, and is usually a question of good fortune—if it takes place at all. It will almost certainly not occur if the young cider has been sulfated as a matter of course in suppressing spoilage agents prior to storage. Today, it is possible to purchase malolactic bacteria cultures and, if you wish to try to bring about this fermentation deliberately, then you will need to add the culture along with nutrients to the young racked-off cider and bring it into a warmer environment for a period.

Appendix 4

USING THE HYDROMETER

A hydrometer measures the specific gravity (SG) of a liquid. Used in making beer, wine, and cider, a hydrometer offers an approximate measure of the dissolved sugars and the potential alcohol obtainable from those sugars.

The SG of the natural juice (or wort/must in the case of beer/wine) is sometimes referred to as the original gravity (OG). The hydrometer can do no better than offer us approximate measures of the sugar and potential alcohol, because all the other dissolved materials—the acids, the developing alcohol, the suspended proteins of the yeast and apples—and not just the sugar, make their individual contributions to the measured SG. However, the hydrometer works because the dissolved sugar is by far and away the principal contributor to the measured SG.

Most cidermaking never involves, or needs to involve, a hydrometer. The eye, watching out for all the indicators marking the progress of fermentation, and the practice of tasting the cider at appropriate stages are, in the long run, probably better judges than a hydrometer. However, the instrument has its uses, and some people like to have a quantitative measure of the fermentation progress and the formed alcohol.

A hydrometer can:

- Indicate the approximate level of sugars in the original pressed juice and therefore, by reading the scale, the potential alcohol obtainable from these natural sugars alone assuming complete fermentation
- Provide the quantity of (white) sugar to be added in order to achieve a particular alcoholic strength
- Show the SG of the final fermented-out cider and the approximate residual sugar (tiny remaining unfermented quantities) in the cider
- Approximate the alcoholic strength of the final cider by deducting the final sugar level from the total sugars (comprised of the original plus the added) and reading off the % alcohol scale

An example:

If our OG happened to be 1060 = 1 lb. 9 oz. (708 g.) sugar per 5 quarts (4.5 liters)

Added sugar at racked off stage = 6 oz. (170 g.) sugar per 5 quarts (4.5 liters)

Total possible fermentable sugar = 1 lb. 15 oz. (878 g.) sugar per 5 quarts (4.5 liters)

Suppose final SG to be 1005 = 1 oz. (28 g.) sugar per 5 quarts (4.5 liters)

Total sugar actually fermented = 1 lb. 14 oz. (850 g.) sugar per 5 quarts (4.5 liters)

Final alcoholic strength of cider = 9.5%

Our final cider is likely to have a percent alcohol by volume (abv) measure of less than this, because we didn't take into account the slight volume changes upon racking, but nevertheless, this is quite a strong cider—not surprising, because the juice we started with in this example at SG 1060 must have been very sweet.

Taking readings off a hydrometer are notoriously difficult, and if you intend to use the instrument, it is better simply to accept approximate readings than to struggle for greater accuracy and end up both defeated and exhausted. You will need a tall narrow-diameter clear-walled specimen vessel of a height greater than the length of the hydrometer. Glass measuring cylinders are the best pieces of apparatus, though improvising one of these from a clear plastic fruit juice bottle is possible. Readings should be taken from the bottom of the meniscus— if you can even see the meniscus—for therein lies the basic problem of taking readings. Don't worry. Cidermaking, like most of the best things in life, is actually a craft that is best exercised through use of all the senses, along with developing judgments and experience.

Siphon off the juice or cider you wish to measure into the thoroughly clean and dry specimen vessel, more or less up to the top. Lower the hydrometer carefully into the liquid, restrain it from rotating and touching the sides of the vessel, wait for it to remain perfectly still, and then read off the SG. Return the juice/cider to the fermentation vessel. Rinse and dry both specimen vessel and hydrometer.

Approximate SG values to prospective alcoholic strengths are given on page 49.

Appendix 5

PASTEURIZATION AND STABILIZATION

Pasteurization has already been dealt with in the context of preserving apple juice for drinking. However, it is also often used as a stabilizing treatment for cider (and perry), the practice being a vexing question among cidermakers.

Purists won't do it, placing it in the same category as sulfating and the question of additives, including the use of cultured yeasts and the role of white sugar and other artificial sweeteners. Indeed, among many cidermakers, the definition of real cider revolves around these issues. The anguishing to some extent is perfectly understandable, given that commercial ciders can be subject to some grisly practices.

For others, who would consider themselves to be perfectly genuine small-scale traditional cidermakers, pasteurization represents a reliable and safe means of rendering their ciders completely stable, and is usually used in conjunction with artificial conditioning (carbonation) of their ciders, especially medium-sweet/sweet ciders. For such makers, especially if they are retailing the product, there are clear advantages to this approach. Naturally conditioned medium-sweet/sweet ciders that are live, in deliberately having tiny amounts of yeast in the bottle, do run a small risk of burst bottles, a possibility that will increase the longer the bottle remains unopened. If the bottle remains on a shelf unsold for some considerable period, there is a palpable risk. Indeed, any traditional hazy cider, perhaps retaining trace quantities of yeast, is potentially unstable and runs a risk that can be removed by pasteurization. Good-quality pasteurizers of various capacities are available from reputable commercial suppliers.

Of course, some cider producers, large and small, obviate the need for pasteurization when making a medium-sweet/sweet cider by sweetening a dry cider with saccharine, aspartame, sorbitol, or lactose, all of which are not fermentable, a practice that is an abomination to purists. Against such considerations is the fact there can be no question that pasteurization does alter (and to our minds, impair) the flavor of the cider. For the small-scale maker of cider for domestic or social use, there is probably simply no need ever to get involved with the process. The small-scale retailer will have to decide on the merits and demerits.

The traditional means of stabilizing cider (still used by many cidermakers today) is simply to store it in bulk long enough and in a cold enough environment before finally racking off from any residual lees. This applies equally to dry cider as to any other cider retaining a residual sweetness. The possibility of re-fermentation, however, is always there in the back of the mind, which is why many cidermakers prefer to pasteurize.

Alternatively, either sulfur dioxide as metabisulfite or Campden tablets equivalent to 100 ppm (2 Campden tablets per 5 quarts, 4.5 liters) can be used to kill any yeast present. A further alternative is to add 1 Campden tablet with a pinch of potassium sorbate per 5 quarts (4.5 liters), a mixture that is sometimes sold as a proprietary stopping compound. There are others also retailed.

Appendix 6
A NOTE ON PATULIN

Patulin is a natural toxin produced by various molds that infect apples and is found in other moldy fruits. The recommended level in pressed apple juice is 50 parts per billion (ppb). Although the toxin is destroyed during fermentation so that cider itself is free of patulin, it is still advisable to observe the precautions outlined below anyway. Observing the precautions below is essential in the case of any unfermented juice or juice products made for personal consumption or those being retailed.

Although most of the patulin is found in the moldy part of an apple, even the sound-looking adjacent parts may be infected with the toxin. For this reason, it is recommended that any apple being used to make juice or cider that shows evidence of mold should be discarded. Any adjacent apples that have spent any time in contact with moldy fruit should also be discarded, even if they appear to be sound. Bruised apples, on the other hand, are not necessarily infected at all, though damaged flesh immediately is more open to mold attack. If you have a superabundance of apples and wish to be cautious, then discard bruised fruit. Otherwise, use your judgment. If the fruit is deeply bruised, discard it, if recently and lightly bruised, you will probably wish to use it. The above levels of patulin are only guidelines, and there is no cheap test available to determine the levels of patulin in juice, although some are currently in development.

Patulin has always been with us—we have always had moldy apples. There is no need to become alarmist about it. For many of us, we probably take in higher concentrations of pollutants every time we take a breath in some city environments, or when we take a glass of water from our domestic water supply. Yes, the particular toxin in moldy fruit has been identified, given a name, and some of its effects investigated enough for us to be aware we should minimize its levels in such things as natural apple products. The truth, however, is that we will probably never be able to remove patulin entirely from apple juice and ciders.

Observe the following code:

- Discard apples that are in any way moldy or have been in contact with moldy apples.
- Wash apples thoroughly before extracting juice from them.

The apples here are infected with a variety of molds and should not be used for either juice or cidermaking.

Appendix 7

CLEANING/STERILIZING WOODEN VESSELS

Cleaning and sterilizing wooden vessels requires special consideration to make certain they are fit for fermentation and storage of cider. A number of options are available depending on the type of cask under consideration.

New Casks

Wash out new casks with several gallons of warm water. Make up brine by dissolving 8 oz. (227 g.) salt in 40 fl. oz. (1183 ml.) of hot water for a 25-quart (22.5 liter) barrel, increasing the quantity for higher volumes. Add the brine to the barrel and fill it up with hot water (do not use boiling water, because it can open up staves). Leave for a week, open up, and rinse out well with cold water until free of salt.

Soiled Casks

1) Remove any gross dirt/deposit on the inside of barrels by adding several handfuls of small stone chippings or a length of brass chain. Fill with hot water and shake thoroughly and repeatedly. Remove chain. In the case of stone chippings, remove by repeated swilling out with hot water.

2) Make up a solution of sodium carbonate (washing soda) at the rate of 4 oz. (125 g.) to every 5 quarts (4.5 liters) of cold water. For larger barrels, you will probably need to make up about 100 quarts (95 liters) of this solution.

3) Pour the soda solution into the barrel, bung tightly, and slosh around at regular intervals over the next two days.

4) Empty and rinse out thoroughly with copious quantities of cold water.

5) Prepare a solution of citric acid at the rate of 1 oz. (28 g.) to every 5 quarts (4.5 liters) of cold water. Add this in sufficient volume to the barrels to neutralize any residual sodium carbonate. Swirl around thoroughly.

6) Drain and rinse thoroughly with copious quantities of water.

7) Drain, dry, and bung up for a week.

8) Make up a sterilizing solution of ⅒ oz. (3 g.) sodium or potassium metabisulfite (or 6 Campden tablets) with ¼ oz. (10 g.) citric acid dissolved in 20 fl. oz. (591 ml.) of water. Be careful—this solution releases a lot of sulfur dioxide, which should not be inhaled.

9) Add this solution to the barrel, bung, and swirl solution round. Keep barrel bunged until required for use.

10) Rinse out barrel with copious quantities of cold water, after which your vessel will be sweet and sterile and ready for use.

As an alternative to the use of sodium carbonate as the cleaning agent, sodium hypochlorite as the active ingredient in domestic bleach can also be used. Make up a solution by dissolving 1 fl. oz. (28 ml.) of domestic bleach in 5 quarts (4.5 liters) of cold water. Use this in the above sequence instead of the sodium carbonate, but otherwise follow the procedure.

Steam Treatment of Barrels

An additional method of treating particularly soiled barrels is to steam treat them. First, rinse out the barrel with boiling water, but keep this moving in order to prevent an opening of the staves. Steam clean the barrel by connecting a plastic or rubber pipe to a pressure cooker. Remove the pressure relief valve, connect the pipe, and steam for about thirty minutes by putting the pipe through the bunghole. After this, rinse well with hot water, and then either treat with salt as above, or with a sterilizing solution, finally rinsing out with copious quantities of cold water.

This may seem like a rather complicated process, but while wood is an excellent material to have for cider vessels, it is prone to getting dirty and infected. Old barrels will particularly need the above treatment. Don't forget to use your nose to finally gauge the sweetness of your barrels after the above cleaning and sterilization. If something is still not quite right and there is still a little mustiness or sourness there, you will need to repeat the procedure.

Don't immediately sniff at vessels to check for sweetness after the use of sulfating agents—use your nose only at the end of the final rinsing session.

Barrels not being used for any length of time should be stored with a pint or so of metabisulfite/citric acid solution (step 8). Rinse this out thoroughly with cold water when the barrel is about to be used again. This ensures the inside of the barrel remains sterile and sweet.

Barrels that have recently contained rum, brandy, or sherry are to be prized, since cider stored in these acquires special vintage characteristics. Such barrels should not be cleaned out for obvious reasons.

To increase the lifetime of barrels and to prevent their drying out with consequent loss of cider, the exterior can be treated with linseed oil, say, every three years or so.

More Books from Fox Chapel Publishing

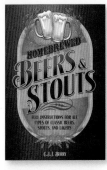

Homebrewed Beers & Stouts
Full Instructions for All Types of Classic Beers, Stouts, and Lagers
By C. J. J. Berry

Learn how to create light summer ales, pale lagers, or an authentic stout with over 70 recipes for brewing your own beer at home.

ISBN: 978-1-56523-601-1
$14.95 · 160 Pages

Big Book of Brewing
The Classic Guide to All-Grain Brewing
By Dave Line

Brewing your own beer is easier than you think with the easy-to-follow instructions in this book that will teach you the simple "mashing" technique that produces the finest flavored beers, ales, stouts, and lagers.

ISBN: 978-1-56523-603-5
$17.95 · 216 Pages

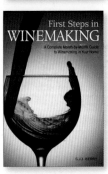

First Steps in Winemaking
A Complete Month-by-Month Guide to Winemaking in Your Home
By C. J. J. Berry

Delve into the world of at-home winemaking with methods and techniques that will turn your kitchen into a vineyard.

ISBN: 978-1-56523-602-8
$14.95 · 232 Pages

130 New Winemaking Recipes
Make Delicious Wine at Home Using Fruits, Grains, and Herbs
By C. J. J. Berry

Follow these 130 classic recipes for making wine in your own kitchen using traditional country ingredients.

ISBN: 978-1-56523-600-4
$12.95 · 136 Pages